Also by Elinor Wylie
COLLECTED PROSE
designed by W. A. Dwiggins

LAST POEMS
designed by W. A. Dwiggins

*

"Her work . . . had the seal of a liveliness upon
it, and a perfection like those Egyptian crowns
whose fragile but enduring beauty preserves the
fine essence of a life proudly lived more surely
than the pyramids."
— *The Saturday Review of Literature*

*

THESE ARE BORZOI BOOKS, PUBLISHED BY
ALFRED·A·KNOPF

COLLECTED POEMS

OF

ELINOR WYLIE

Collected Poems

OF

ELINOR WYLIE

Alfred A. Knopf, New York

1977

Published May 20, 1932
Reprinted fourteen times
Sixteenth printing, July 1977

THIS IS A BORZOI BOOK,
PUBLISHED BY ALFRED A. KNOPF, INC.

Manufactured in the United States of America

FOREWORD

THE contents of this book embody the contents of Elinor Wylie's four books of poems, *Nets to Catch the Wind* (1921), *Black Armour* (1923), *Trivial Breath* (1928), and *Angels and Earthly Creatures* (1929), in the exact sequence and order in which they were originally published. Added to these is a section of poems hitherto uncollected in book form, some of which have previously been published in periodicals. A few, on the other hand, have never before been printed. The editor has felt deeply the responsibility of including in a volume by this poet no work of whose inclusion she might not have approved. Owing to many considerations, however, it seemed judicious to gather within the same covers the best of her work in verse that any exact bibliography will show reposing in magazine files. And, in a sifting and re-sifting of the poetry she left behind in manuscript, certain other writings also seemed to merit inclusion. All these I have arranged in an order as nearly chronological as was possible. Most remarkable among the manuscripts is an unfinished ballad describing the poet's flight from man to seek sanctuary amid the brute creation. It is a poem the poet kept by her for years and had hoped to finish. She left another poem, not printed here, in the metrical form she made famous in "Peregrine," namely "The Golden Heifer." It is, superficially at least, light in tone, but she never, I think, worked it out completely in her mind. I have included, from among the work done when she was writing most of the poems in *Black Armour*, a flight of poetic prose entitled "The Heart's Desire," an experiment that she for some time set store by, and one which seems to me quite an extraordinary spontaneous expression. "The Madwoman's Miracle" likewise dates from this time, as does "Peregrine's Sunday Song."

Of the later poems it is obvious that (to mention only two) "The Pebble" and "Little Eclogue" are sufficiently remarkable, while the beautiful song, "A Tear for Cressid," illustrates one characteristic of the poet: namely that she not infrequently wrote songs which went to a tune of her own devising. There were several such of which she was fond, too casual and intimate to include here; but I can vividly recall her singing the Cressid song to me after she had composed it. The tune she had made for it greatly took her fancy.

Such mention leads me to say a word concerning the lighter verse that, in intervals of writing poetry, Elinor could shape so deftly and wittily, principally for the entertainment of her intimate friends, though she occasionally gave it to the "columns" of Christopher Morley and of "F. P. A." The most brilliant instance is the portrait of herself, in verse, which she wrote for the *New Yorker's* series of "Profiles," and which they reprinted after her death "in memory of a lovely person." With the generosity that was always hers she stresses in it what she conceives to be her foibles. Naturally she distorts the image, though the peculiarities of her nature are recognizable — peculiarities, one may say here, that only served to make that nature the more enchanting. Her mind, need it be said, had an excessive liveliness of apprehension. She could range "from grave to gay, from lively to severe" in the space, it seemed, of an instant. Before me, as I write, lie certain mere rhymes such as she would constantly fashion about some small circumstance, among them a humorous "Cri du Cœur," two verses of which run

> My books lie on the sofa
> And I lie on the floor:
> I wish that I might loaf a
> Little minute more.

> My thoughts refuse to mingle, and
> I'm murdered by fatigue,
> So I think I'll go to England
> And join the Primrose League.

Yet, quite naturally, what might be termed by some a mere facetious triviality reminds me here principally of the unsparing intensity she gave to her work, despite a precarious constitution. She immediately follows the above with five lines on another sheet of paper purposely entitled "Creed du Cœur," which brings her vividly before me in one of her most delightful moods:

> I'd rather be silly and kind
> Than graciously cool and refined;
> The second shows poise
> And a musical voice,
> But the first shows a generous mind.

Here are, among other fragments, charades written for friends, a sonnet satirizing the vogue of the Japanese "hokku" form, once a fad with certain poets, and eight lines advising the lovelorn that

> if you hunger for a kiss,
> Take it, but go without your dinner,

"lest," she characteristically remarks, "intellect should be submerged." There is a discussion in verse as to just why, in friendship, "all her geese are swans." There is a long set of verses entitled "Ribald Rhapsody," which is not ribald at all and is supplemented by an again utterly characteristic "Partial List of the Literary and Historical References Contained in the Foregoing." Lastly there is her own version of Hadrian's Address to his Soul, followed by "Milord Byron's Translation." Here is Elinor Wylie's:

> Little soul, like a cloud, like a feather,
> My body's small guest and companion,
> Where now do you rest, in what places—
> Stripped naked, and rigid, and pallid,
> Do you play as before, little jester?

In bearing witness to this more frivolous—and yet hardly so frivolous, after all—side of one I deeply love and whom I have always esteemed a genius, I will not be misunderstood by anyone who really knew Elinor. It is the casual, the fragmentary, the apparently inconsequential that touch the heart to the quick when a great and noble spirit, also so beautifully human, is gone. And all her friends knew Elinor's lively, witty side, her childlikeness, her headlong sympathies, the impulsive traits that endeared. Erudite and the paragon of artistic integrity, she could flash into a mood of clever nonsense at any moment, or exclaim with an apparent abandon of admiration over some bijouterie or some apt phrase coined by another. Her bronze hair seemed to have wings, and her head on its beautiful throat to bear the face of one flying. Often tense with actual physical pain, her lineaments in laughter had both the surprised innocence and the mischief of a child. She loved old Scotch and Irish ballads and songs, and sang them in a high-pitched wistful way that I shall never forget. But I have been led far afield, and I am particularly reminded of this by a neat typewritten quotation which she inserted among her papers:

> "But Protagoras," I added, "if you have no objection, I should like to drop these criticisms on songs and poems. . . . For, I must confess, I think that talking about poetry bears a close resemblance to the festive amusements of the vulgar and uneducated."

I do not contend, far less would she, that the poems now first collected here are in the same category with her final sonnets or the best lyrics in her last, posthumous book. They are, however, of vital interest in a further exposition of her nature, a nature composed of many fascinating elements, all of which were fused at white heat into great art in her best work. In eight years she produced eight books, four of prose and four of poetry, all wrought at her highest pitch, all preserving her indelible signature. "Ah, what avails the sceptred race!"

WILLIAM ROSE BENÉT

New York City
  December 1, 1931.

CONTENTS

NETS TO CATCH THE WIND

BLACK ARMOUR

I. BREASTPLATE

II. GAUNTLET

TRIVIAL BREATH

I

II

ANGELS AND EARTHLY
CREATURES

I ONE PERSON

II. ELEMENTS AND ANGELS

HITHERTO UNCOLLECTED POEMS

LIST OF ILLUSTRATIONS

NETS TO CATCH THE WIND

Beauty

Say not of Beauty she is good,
Or aught but beautiful,
Or sleek to doves' wings of the wood
Her wild wings of a gull.

Call her not wicked; that word's touch
Consumes her like a curse;
But love her not too much, too much,
For that is even worse.

O, she is neither good nor bad,
But innocent and wild!
Enshrine her and she dies, who had
The hard heart of a child.

The Eagle and the Mole

Avoid the reeking herd,
Shun the polluted flock,
Live like that stoic bird,
The eagle of the rock.

The huddled warmth of crowds
Begets and fosters hate;
He keeps, above the clouds,
His cliff inviolate.

When flocks are folded warm,
And herds to shelter run,
He sails above the storm,
He stares into the sun.

If in the eagle's track
Your sinews cannot leap,
Avoid the lathered pack,
Turn from the steaming sheep.

If you would keep your soul
From spotted sight or sound,
Live like the velvet mole;
Go burrow underground.

And there hold intercourse
With roots of trees and stones,
With rivers at their source,
And disembodied bones.

Madman's Song

Better to see your cheek grown hollow,
Better to see your temple worn,
Than to forget to follow, follow,
After the sound of a silver horn.

Better to bind your brow with willow
And follow, follow until you die,
Than to sleep with your head on a golden pillow,
Nor lift it up when the hunt goes by.

Better to see your cheek grown sallow
And your hair grown gray, so soon, so soon,
Than to forget to hallo, hallo,
After the milk-white hounds of the moon.

The Prinkin' Leddie

"The Hielan' lassies are a' for spinnin',
The Lowlan' lassies for prinkin' and pinnin';
My daddie w'u'd chide me, an' so w'u'd my minnie
If I s'u'd bring hame sic a prinkin' leddie."

Now haud your tongue, ye haverin' coward,
For whilst I'm young I'll go flounced an' flowered,
In lutestring striped like the strings o' a fiddle,
Wi' gowden girdles aboot my middle.

In your Hielan' glen, where the rain pours steady,
Ye'll be gay an' glad for a prinkin' leddie;
Where the rocks are all bare an' the turf is all sodden,
An' lassies gae sad in their homespun an' hodden.

My silks are stiff wi' patterns o' siller,
I've an ermine hood like the hat o' a miller,
I've chains o' coral like rowan berries,
An' a cramoisie mantle that cam' frae Paris.

Ye'll be glad for the glint o' its scarlet linin'
When the larks are up an' the sun is shinin';
When the winds are up an' ower the heather
Your heart'll be gay wi' my gowden feather.

When the skies are low an' the earth is frozen,
Ye'll be gay an' glad for the leddie ye've chosen,
When ower the snow I go prinkin' an' prancin'
In my wee red slippers were made for dancin'.

6

It's better a leddie like Solomon's lily
Than one that'll run like a Hielan' gillie
A-linkin' it ower the leas, my laddie,
In a raggedy kilt an' a belted plaidie!

August

Why should this Negro insolently stride
Down the red noonday on such noiseless feet?
Piled in his barrow, tawnier than wheat,
Lie heaps of smouldering daisies, sombre-eyed,
Their copper petals shrivelled up with pride,
Hot with a superfluity of heat,
Like a great brazier borne along the street
By captive leopards, black and burning pied.

Are there no water-lilies, smooth as cream,
With long stems dripping crystal? Are there none
Like those white lilies, luminous and cool,
Plucked from some hemlock-darkened northern
     stream
By fair-haired swimmers, diving where the sun
Scarce warms the surface of the deepest pool?

The Crooked Stick

First Traveller: What's that lying in the dust?

Second Traveller: A crooked stick.

First Traveller: What's it worth, if you can trust
   To arithmetic?

Second Traveller: Isn't this a riddle?

First Traveller: No, a trick.

Second Traveller: It's worthless. Leave it where it lies.

First Traveller: Wait; count ten;
   Rub a little dust upon your eyes;
   Now, look again.

Second Traveller: Well, and what the devil is it, then?

First Traveller: It's the sort of crooked stick that shepherds
   know.

Second Traveller: Someone's loss!

First Traveller: Bend it, and you make of it a bow.
   Break it, a cross.

Second Traveller: But it's all grown over with moss!

Atavism

I always was afraid of Somes's Pond:
Not the little pond, by which the willow stands,
Where laughing boys catch alewives in their hands
In brown, bright shallows; but the one beyond.
There, when the frost makes all the birches burn
Yellow as cow-lilies, and the pale sky shines
Like a polished shell between black spruce and pines,
Some strange thing tracks us, turning where we turn.

You'll say I dream it, being the true daughter
Of those who in old times endured this dread.
Look! Where the lily-stems are showing red
A silent paddle moves below the water,
A sliding shape has stirred them like a breath;
Tall plumes surmount a painted mask of death.

Wild Peaches

I

When the world turns completely upside down
You say we'll emigrate to the Eastern Shore
Aboard a river-boat from Baltimore;
We'll live among wild peach trees, miles from town,
You'll wear a coonskin cap, and I a gown
Homespun, dyed butternut's dark gold colour.
Lost, like your lotus-eating ancestor,
We'll swim in milk and honey till we drown.

The winter will be short, the summer long,
The autumn amber-hued, sunny and hot,
Tasting of cider and of scuppernong;
All seasons sweet, but autumn best of all.
The squirrels in their silver fur will fall
Like falling leaves, like fruit, before your shot.

2

The autumn frosts will lie upon the grass
Like bloom on grapes of purple-brown and gold.
The misted early mornings will be cold;
The little puddles will be roofed with glass.
The sun, which burns from copper into brass,
Melts these at noon, and makes the boys unfold
Their knitted mufflers; full as they can hold,
Fat pockets dribble chestnuts as they pass.

Peaches grow wild, and pigs can live in clover;
A barrel of salted herrings lasts a year;
The spring begins before the winter's over.
By February you may find the skins
Of garter snakes and water moccasins
Dwindled and harsh, dead-white and cloudy-clear.

3

When April pours the colours of a shell
Upon the hills, when every little creek
Is shot with silver from the Chesapeake
In shoals new-minted by the ocean swell,
When strawberries go begging, and the sleek
Blue plums lie open to the blackbird's beak,
We shall live well—we shall live very well.

The months between the cherries and the peaches
Are brimming cornucopias which spill
Fruits red and purple, sombre-bloomed and black;
Then, down rich fields and frosty river beaches
We'll trample bright persimmons, while you kill
Bronze partridge, speckled quail, and canvasback.

4

Down to the Puritan marrow of my bones
There's something in this richness that I hate.
I love the look, austere, immaculate,
Of landscapes drawn in pearly monotones.
There's something in my very blood that owns
Bare hills, cold silver on a sky of slate,
A thread of water, churned to milky spate
Streaming through slanted pastures fenced with stones.

I love those skies, thin blue or snowy gray,
Those fields sparse-planted, rendering meagre sheaves;
That spring, briefer than apple-blossom's breath,
Summer, so much too beautiful to stay,
Swift autumn, like a bonfire of leaves,
And sleepy winter, like the sleep of death.

Sanctuary

This is the bricklayer; hear the thud
Of his heavy load dumped down on stone.
His lustrous bricks are brighter than blood,
His smoking mortar whiter than bone.

Set each sharp-edged, fire-bitten brick
Straight by the plumb-line's shivering length;
Make my marvellous wall so thick
Dead nor living may shake its strength.

Full as a crystal cup with drink
Is my cell with dreams, and quiet, and cool. . . .
Stop, old man! You must leave a chink;
How can I breathe? *You can't, you fool!*

The Lion and the Lamb

I saw a Tiger's golden flank,
I saw what food he ate,
By a desert spring he drank;
The Tiger's name was Hate.

Then I saw a placid Lamb
Lying fast asleep;
Like a river from its dam
Flashed the Tiger's leap.

I saw a Lion tawny-red,
Terrible and brave;
The Tiger's leap overhead
Broke like a wave.

In sand below or sun above
He faded like a flame.
The Lamb said, "I am Love;
Lion, tell your name."

The Lion's voice thundering
Shook his vaulted breast,
"I am Love. By this spring,
Brother, let us rest."

The Church-Bell

As I was lying in my bed
I heard the church-bell ring;
Before one solemn word was said
A bird began to sing.

I heard a dog begin to bark
And a bold crowing cock;
The bell, between the cold and dark,
Tolled. It was five o'clock.

The church-bell tolled, and the bird sang,
A clear true voice he had;
The cock crew, and the church-bell rang,
I knew it had gone mad.

A hand reached down from the dark skies,
It took the bell-rope thong,
The bell cried "Look! Lift up your eyes!"
The clapper shook to song.

The iron clapper laughed aloud,
Like clashing wind and wave;
The bell cried out "Be strong and proud!"
Then, with a shout, "Be brave!"

The rumbling of the market-carts,
The pounding of men's feet
Were drowned in song; "Lift up your hearts!"
The sound was loud and sweet.

Slow and slow the great bell swung,
It hung in the steeple mute;
And people tore its living tongue
Out by the very root.

A Crowded Trolley Car

The rain's cold grains are silver-gray
Sharp as golden sands,
A bell is clanging, people sway
Hanging by their hands.

Supple hands, or gnarled and stiff,
Snatch and catch and grope;
That face is yellow-pale, as if
The fellow swung from rope.

Dull like pebbles, sharp like knives,
Glances strike and glare,
Fingers tangle, Bluebeard's wives
Dangle by the hair.

Orchard of the strangest fruits
Hanging from the skies;
Brothers, yet insensate brutes
Who fear each other's eyes.

One man stands as free men stand,
As if his soul might be
Brave, unbroken; see his hand
Nailed to an oaken tree.

Bells in the Rain

Sleep falls, with limpid drops of rain,
Upon the steep cliffs of the town.
Sleep falls; men are at peace again
While the small drops fall softly down.

The bright drops ring like bells of glass
Thinned by the wind, and lightly blown;
Sleep cannot fall on peaceful grass
So softly as it falls on stone.

Peace falls unheeded on the dead
Asleep; they have had deep peace to drink;
Upon a live man's bloody head
It falls most tenderly, I think.

Winter Sleep

When against earth a wooden heel
Clicks as loud as stone and steel,
When snow turns flour instead of flakes,
And frost bakes clay as fire bakes,
When the hard-bitten fields at last
Crack like iron flawed in the cast,
When the world is wicked and cross and old,
I long to be quit of the cruel cold.

Little birds like bubbles of glass
Fly to other Americas,
Birds as bright as sparkles of wine
Fly in the night to the Argentine,
Birds of azure and flame-birds go
To the tropical Gulf of Mexico:
They chase the sun, they follow the heat,
It is sweet in their bones, O sweet, sweet, sweet!
It's not with them that I'd love to be,
But under the roots of the balsam tree.

Just as the spiniest chestnut-burr
Is lined within with the finest fur,
So the stony-walled, snow-roofed house
Of every squirrel and mole and mouse
Is lined with thistledown, sea-gull's feather,
Velvet mullein-leaf, heaped together
With balsam and juniper, dry and curled,
Sweeter than anything else in the world.

O what a warm and darksome nest
Where the wildest things are hidden to rest!
It's there that I'd love to lie and sleep,
Soft, soft, soft, and deep, deep, deep!

Village Mystery

The woman in the pointed hood
And cloak blue-gray like a pigeon's wing,
Whose orchard climbs to the balsam-wood,
Has done a cruel thing.

To her back door-step came a ghost,
A girl who had been ten years dead,
She stood by the granite hitching-post
And begged for a piece of bread.

Now why should I, who walk alone,
Who am ironical and proud,
Turn, when a woman casts a stone
At a beggar in a shroud?

I saw the dead girl cringe and whine,
And cower in the weeping air—
But, oh, she was no kin of mine,
And so I did not care!

Sunset on the Spire

All that I dream
   By day or night
Lives in that stream
   Of lovely light.
Here is the earth,
   And there is the spire;
This is my hearth,
   And that is my fire.
From the sun's dome
   I am shouted proof
That this is my home,
   And that is my roof.
Here is my food,
   And here is my drink,
And I am wooed
   From the moon's brink.
And the days go over,
   And the nights end;
Here is my lover,
   Here is my friend.
All that I
   Could ever ask
Wears that sky
   Like a thin gold mask.

Escape

When foxes eat the last gold grape,
And the last white antelope is killed,
I shall stop fighting and escape
Into a little house I'll build.

But first I'll shrink to fairy size,
With a whisper no one understands,
Making blind moons of all your eyes,
And muddy roads of all your hands.

And you may grope for me in vain
In hollows under the mangrove root,
Or where, in apple-scented rain,
The silver wasp-nests hang like fruit.

The Fairy Goldsmith

'Here's a wonderful thing,
A humming-bird's wing
　　In hammered gold,
And store well chosen
Of snowflakes frozen
　　In crystal cold.

Black onyx cherries
And mistletoe berries
　　Of chrysoprase,
Jade buds, tight shut,
All carven and cut
　　In intricate ways.

Here, if you please
Are little gilt bees
　　In amber drops
Which look like honey,
Translucent and sunny,
　　From clover-tops.

Here's an elfin girl
Of mother-of-pearl
　　And moonshine made,
With tortoise-shell hair
Both dusky and fair
　　In its light and shade.

Here's lacquer laid thin,
Like a scarlet skin

On an ivory fruit;
And a filigree frost
Of frail notes lost
    From a fairy lute.

Here's a turquoise chain
Of sun-shower rain
    To wear if you wish;
And glimmering green
With aquamarine,
    A silvery fish.

Here are pearls all strung
On a thread among
    Pretty pink shells;
And bubbles blown
From the opal stone
    Which ring like bells.

Touch them and take them,
But do not break them!
    Beneath your hand
They will wither like foam
If you carry them home
    Out of fairy-land.

O, they never can last
Though you hide them fast
    From moth and from rust;
In your monstrous day
They will crumble away
    Into quicksilver dust.

"Fire and Sleet and Candlelight"

For this you've striven
    Daring, to fail:
Your sky is riven
    Like a tearing veil.

For this, you've wasted
    Wings of your youth;
Divined, and tasted
    Bitter springs of truth.

From sand unslakèd
    Twisted strong cords,
And wandered naked
    Among trysted swords.

There's a word unspoken,
    A knot untied.
Whatever is broken
    The earth may hide.

The road was jagged
    Over sharp stones:
Your body's too ragged
    To cover your bones.

The wind scatters
    Tears upon dust;
Your soul's in tatters
    Where the spears thrust.

Your race is ended—
See, it is run:
Nothing is mended
Under the sun.

Straight as an arrow
You fall to a sleep
Not too narrow
And not too deep.

Blood Feud

Once, when my husband was a child, there came
To his father's table, one who called him kin,
In sunbleached corduroys paler than his skin.
His look was grave and kind; he bore the name
Of the dead singer of Senlac, and his smile.
Shyly and courteously he smiled and spoke;
"I've been in the laurel since the winter broke;
Four months, I reckon; yes, sir, quite a while."

He'd killed a score of foemen in the past,
In some blood feud, a dark and monstrous thing;
To him it seemed his duty.   At the last
His enemies found him by a forest spring,
Which, as he died, lay bright beneath his head,
A silver shield that slowly turned to red.

Sea Lullaby

The old moon is tarnished
With smoke of the flood,
The dead leaves are varnished
With colour like blood,

A treacherous smiler
With teeth white as milk,
A savage beguiler
In sheathings of silk,

The sea creeps to pillage,
She leaps on her prey;
A child of the village
Was murdered today.

She came up to meet him
In a smooth golden cloak,
She choked him and beat him
To death, for a joke.

Her bright locks were tangled,
She shouted for joy,
With one hand she strangled
A strong little boy.

Now in silence she lingers
Beside him all night
To wash her long fingers
In silvery light.

30

Nancy

You are a rose, but set with sharpest spine;
You are a pretty bird that pecks at me;
You are a little squirrel on a tree,
Pelting me with the prickly fruit of the pine;
A diamond, torn from a crystal mine,
Not like that milky treasure of the sea,
A smooth, translucent pearl, but skilfully
Carven to cut, and faceted to shine.

If you are flame, it dances and burns blue;
If you are light, it pierces like a star
Intenser than a needlepoint of ice.
The dexterous touch that shaped the soul of you,
Mingled, to mix, and make you what you are,
Magic between the sugar and the spice.

A Proud Lady

Hate in the world's hand
Can carve and set its seal
Like the strong blast of sand
Which cuts into steel.

I have seen how the finger of hate
Can mar and mould
Faces burned passionate
And frozen cold.

Sorrowful faces worn
As stone with rain,
Faces writhing with scorn
And sullen with pain.

But you have a proud face
Which the world cannot harm,
You have turned the pain to a grace
And the scorn to a charm.

You have taken the arrows and slings
Which prick and bruise
And fashioned them into wings
For the heels of your shoes.

From the world's hand which tries
To tear you apart
You have stolen the falcon's eyes
And the lion's heart.

What has it done, this world,
With hard finger-tips,
But sweetly chiselled and curled
Your inscrutable lips?

The Tortoise in Eternity

Within my house of patterned horn
I sleep in such a bed
As men may keep before they're born
And after they are dead.

Sticks and stones may break their bones,
And words may make them bleed;
There is not one of them who owns
An armour to his need.

Tougher than hide or lozenged bark,
Snow-storm and thunder proof,
And quick with sun, and thick with dark,
Is this my darling roof.

Men's troubled dreams of death and birth
Pulse mother-o'-pearl to black;
I bear the rainbow bubble Earth
Square on my scornful back.

Incantation

A white well
In a black cave;
A bright shell
In a dark wave.

A white rose
Black brambles hood;
Smooth bright snows
In a dark wood.

A flung white glove
In a dark fight;
A white dove
On a wild black night.

A white door
In a dark lane;
A bright core
To bitter black pain.

A white hand
Waved from dark walls;
In a burnt black land
Bright waterfalls.

A bright spark
Where black ashes are;
In the smothering dark
One white star.

Silver Filigree

The icicles wreathing
   On trees in festoon
Swing, swayed to our breathing:
   They're made of the moon.

She's a pale, waxen taper;
   And these seem to drip
Transparent as paper
   From the flame of her tip.

Molten, smoking a little,
   Into crystal they pass;
Falling, freezing, to brittle
   And delicate glass.

Each a sharp-pointed flower,
   Each a brief stalactite
Which hangs for an hour
   In the blue cave of night.

AN EARLY PORTRAIT OF
ELINOR WYLIE

From a photograph by Rita Martin

The Falcon

Why should my sleepy heart be taught
To whistle mocking-bird replies?
This is another bird you've caught,
Soft-feathered, with a falcon's eyes.

The bird Imagination,
That flies so far, that dies so soon;
Her wings are coloured like the sun,
Her breast is coloured like the moon.

Weave her a chain of silver twist,
And a little hood of scarlet wool,
And let her perch upon your wrist,
And tell her she is beautiful.

Bronze Trumpets and Sea Water—
on Turning Latin Into English

Alembics turn to stranger things
Strange things, but never while we live
Shall magic turn this bronze that sings
To singing water in a sieve.

The trumpeters of Cæsar's guard
Salute his rigorous bastions
With ordered bruit; the bronze is hard
Though there is silver in the bronze.

Our mutable tongue is like the sea,
Curled wave and shattering thunder-fit;
Dangle in strings of sand shall he
Who smooths the ripples out of it.

Spring Pastoral

Liza, go steep your long white hands
In the cool waters of that spring
Which bubbles up through shiny sands
The colour of a wild-dove's wing.

Dabble your hands, and steep them well
Until those nails are pearly white
Now rosier than a laurel bell;
Then come to me at candlelight.

Lay your cold hands across my brows,
And I shall sleep, and I shall dream
Of silver-pointed willow boughs
Dipping their fingers in a stream.

Velvet Shoes

Let us walk in the white snow
  In a soundless space;
With footsteps quiet and slow,
  At a tranquil pace,
  Under veils of white lace.

I shall go shod in silk,
  And you in wool,
White as a white cow's milk,
  More beautiful
  Than the breast of a gull.

We shall walk through the still town
  In a windless peace;
We shall step upon white down,
  Upon silver fleece,
  Upon softer than these.

We shall walk in velvet shoes:
  Wherever we go
Silence will fall like dews
  On white silence below.
  We shall walk in the snow.

Valentine

Too high, too high to pluck
My heart shall swing.
A fruit no bee shall suck,
No wasp shall sting.

If on some night of cold
It falls to ground
In apple-leaves of gold
I'll wrap it round.

And I shall seal it up
With spice and salt,
In a carven silver cup,
In a deep vault.

Before my eyes are blind
And my lips mute,
I must eat core and rind
Of that same fruit.

Before my heart is dust
At the end of all,
Eat it I must, I must
Were it bitter gall.

But I shall keep it sweet
By some strange art;
Wild honey I shall eat
When I eat my heart.

O honey cool and chaste
As clover's breath!
Sweet Heaven I shall taste
Before my death.

BLACK ARMOUR

I: BREASTPLATE

Full Moon

My bands of silk and miniver
Momently grew heavier;
The black gauze was beggarly thin;
The ermine muffled mouth and chin;
I could not suck the moonlight in.

Harlequin in lozenges
Of love and hate, I walked in these
Striped and ragged rigmaroles;
Along the pavement my footsoles
Trod warily on living coals.

Shouldering the thoughts I loathed,
In their corrupt disguises clothed,
Mortality I could not tear
From my ribs, to leave them bare
Ivory in silver air.

There I walked, and there I raged;
The spiritual savage caged
Within my skeleton, raged afresh
To feel, behind a carnal mesh,
The clean bones crying in the flesh.

Nebuchadnezzar

My body is weary to death of my mischievous brain;
I am weary forever and ever of being brave;
Therefore I crouch on my knees while the cool white
    rain
Curves the clover over my head like a wave.

The stem and the frosty seed of the grass are ripe;
I have devoured their strength; I have drunk them deep;
And the dandelion is gall in a thin green pipe,
But the clover is honey and sun and the smell of sleep.

Three Wishes

Sink out of being, and go down, go down
Through the steep layers of emerald and jade
With warm thin skin of turquoise overlaid,
Where the slow coral spins a ghostly town
Of tower and minaret and fretted crown,
Give up your breath in sleep's subaqueous shade,
Hold to oblivion; are you afraid
Of cold deep death? Are you afraid to drown?

You have three flashing looks, like fairy wishes;
One burns your eyelids with a lightning-wink
Which turns into a rainbow world, and one
Shows sea-birds brighter than the silver fishes,
And one—the last wild chance before you sink—
A flock of dancing clouds about the sun.

Prophecy

I shall lie hidden in a hut
    In the middle of an alder wood,
With the back door blind and bolted shut,
    And the front door locked for good.

I shall lie folded like a saint,
    Lapped in a scented linen sheet,
On a bedstead striped with bright-blue paint,
    Narrow and cold and neat.

The midnight will be glassy black
    Behind the panes, with wind about
To set his mouth against a crack
    And blow the candle out.

Epitaph

For this she starred her eyes with salt
And scooped her temples thin,
Until her face shone pure of fault
From the forehead to the chin.

In coldest crucibles of pain
Her shrinking flesh was fired
And smoothed into a finer grain
To make it more desired.

Pain left her lips more clear than glass;
It coloured and cooled her hand.
She lay a field of scented grass
Yielded as pasture land.

For this her loveliness was curved
And carved as silver is:
For this she was brave: but she deserved
A better grave than this.

Song

It is my thoughts that colour
My soul which slips between;
Thoughts lunar and solar
And gold and sea-green

Tint the pure translucence
Of the crystal thread;
A rainbow nuisance
It runs through my head.

When I am dead, or sleeping
Without any pain,
My soul will stop creeping
Through my jewelled brain.

With no brightness to dye it
None will see where
It flows clear and quiet
As a river of air;

Watering dark places
Without sparkle or sound;
Kissing dumb faces
And the dusty ground.

Drowned Woman

He shall be my jailer
Who sets me free
From shackles frailer
Than the wind-spun sea.

He shall be my teacher
Who cries "Be brave,"
To a weeping creature
In a glass-walled wave.

But he shall be my brother
Whose mocking despair
Dives headlong to smother
In the weeds of my hair.

The Good Birds

Threading the evil hand and look
I sprang, on sinews spare and light,
To sleep beside a water-brook
Where snow was sprinkled overnight.

I spread my cloak upon the ground,
I laid my head upon a stone,
I stared into the sky and found
That I no longer lived alone.

He turned His burning eyes on me
From smoke above a mountain-shelf;
I did not want His company
Who wanted no one but myself.

I whistled shrill, I whistled keen;
The birds were servant to my nod.
They wove their wings into a screen
Between my lovely ground and God.

II: GAUNTLET

Peregrine

Liar and bragger,
He had no friend
Except a dagger
And a candle-end;
The one he read by;
The one scared cravens;
And he was fed by
The Prophet's ravens.
Such haughty creatures
Avoid the human;
They fondle nature's
Breast, not woman—
A she-wolf's puppies—
A wild-cat's pussy-fur:
Their stirrup-cup is
The pride of Lucifer.
A stick he carried,
Slept in a lean-to;
He'd never married,
And he didn't mean to.
He'd tried religion
And found it pleasant;
He relished a pigeon
Stewed with a pheasant
In an iron kettle;
He built stone ovens.
He'd never settle
In any province.
He made pantries

Of Vaux and Arden
And the village gentry's
Kitchen-garden.
Fruits within yards
Were his staples;
He drank whole vineyards
From Rome to Naples,
Then went to Brittany
For the cider.
He could sit any
Horse, a rider
Outstripping Cheiron's
Canter and gallop.
Pau's environs
The pubs of Salop,
Wells and Bath inns
Shared his pleasure
With taverns of Athens;
The Sultan's treasure
He'd seen in Turkey;
He'd known London
Bright and murky.
His bones were sunned on
Paris benches
Beset by sparrows;
Roman trenches,
Cave-men's barrows,
He liked, impartial;
He liked an Abbey.
His step was martial;
Spent and shabby

He wasn't broken;
A dozen lingoes
He must have spoken.
As a king goes
He went, not minding
That he lived seeking
And never finding.
He'd visit Peking
And then be gone soon
To the far Canaries;
He'd cross a monsoon
To chase vagaries.
He loved a city
And a street's alarums;
Parks were pretty
And so were bar-rooms.
He loved fiddles;
He talked with rustics;
Life was riddles
And queer acrostics.
His sins were serried,
His virtues garish;
His corpse was buried
In a country parish.
Before he went hence—
God knows where—
He spoke this sentence
With a princely air:
"The noose draws tighter;
This is the end;
I'm a good fighter,

But a bad friend:
I've played the traitor
Over and over;
I'm a good hater,
But a bad lover."

Heroics

Though here and there a man is left
Whose iron thread eludes the shears,
The martyr with his bosom cleft
Is dead these seven heavy years.

Does he survive whose tongue was slit,
To slake some envy of a king's?
Sportive silver cried from it
Before the savage cut the strings.

The rack has crumpled up the limb
Stretched immediate to fly;
Never ask the end of him
Stubborn to outstare the sky.

Assuming an heroic mask,
He stands a tall derisive tree,
While servile to the speckled task
We move devoted hand and knee.

It is no virtue, but a fault
Thus to breathe ignoble air,
Suffering unclean assault
And insult dubious to bear.

Lucifer Sings in Secret

I am the broken arrow
From Jehovah's quiver;
He will not let me sorrow
Forever and ever.
He will give me a new feather
That is white, not red;
He will bind me together
With the hairs of his head.
My shaft will be jointed
Like the young springing corn;
My tip will be pointed
With a painted thorn.
He will be willing
That I lift my voice,
Among all killing
To make my choice;
To harry the wagons
Of the wicked's retreat;
To murder dragons
Who have licked my feet.
I shall choose the target
His arrow deserves;
I shall trace and mark it
In scarlet curves.
Small and bloody
As a fallen sparrow
My own dead body
Shall receive his arrow.

Preference

These to me are beautiful people;
Thick hair sliding in a ripple;
A tall throat, round as a column;
A mournful mouth, small and solemn,
Having to confound the mourner
Irony in either corner;
The limbs fine, narrow and strong;
Like the wind they walk along,
Like the whirlwind, bad to follow;
The cheekbones high, the cheeks hollow,
The eyes large and wide apart.
They carry a dagger in the heart
So keen and clean it never rankles. . . .
They wear small bones in wrists and ankles.

Simon Gerty

(Who Turned Renegade and Lived with the Indians)

By what appalling dim upheaval
   Demolishing some kinder plan,
Did you become incarnate evil
   Wearing the livery of man?

Perhaps you hated cheeks of tallow,
   Dead eyes, and lineaments of chalk,
Until a beauty came to hallow
   Even the bloodiest tomahawk.

Perhaps you loathed your brothers' features
   Pallid and pinched, or greasy-fat;
Perhaps you loved these alien creatures
   Clean muscled as a panther cat.

Did you believe that being cruel
   Was that which made their foreheads lift
So proudly, gave their eyes a jewel,
   And turned their padding footsteps swift?

As one by one our faiths are shaken
   Our hatreds fall; so mine for you.
Of course I think you were mistaken;
   But still, I see your point of view.

Let No Charitable Hope

Now let no charitable hope
Confuse my mind with images
Of eagle and of antelope:
I am in nature none of these.

I was, being human, born alone;
I am, being woman, hard beset;
I live by squeezing from a stone
The little nourishment I get.

In masks outrageous and austere
The years go by in single file;
But none has merited my fear,
And none has quite escaped my smile.

This Hand

This hand you have observed,
Impassive and detached,
With joints adroitly curved,
And fingers neatly matched:

Blue-veined and yellowish,
Ambiguous to clasp,
And secret as a fish,
And sudden as an asp:

It doubles to a fist,
Or droops composed and chill;
The socket of my wrist
Controls it to my will.

It leaps to my command,
Tautened, or trembling lax;
It lies within your hand
Anatomy of wax.

If I had seen a thorn
Broken to grape-vine bud;
If I had ever borne
Child of our mingled blood;

Elixirs might escape;
But now, compact as stone,
My hand preserves a shape
Too utterly its own.

III: HELMET

Self-portrait

A lens of crystal whose transparence calms
Queer stars to clarity, and disentangles
Fox-fires to form austere refracted angles:
A texture polished on the horny palms
Of vast equivocal creatures, beast or human:
A flint, a substance finer-grained than snow,
Graved with the Graces in intaglio
To set sarcastic sigil on the woman.

This for the mind, and for the little rest
A hollow scooped to blackness in the breast,
The simulacrum of a cloud, a feather:
Instead of stone, instead of sculptured strength,
This soul, this vanity, blown hither and thither
By trivial breath, over the whole world's length.

Cold-blooded Creatures

Man, the egregious egoist
(In mystery the twig is bent),
Imagines, by some mental twist,
That he alone is sentient

Of the intolerable load
Which on all living creatures lies,
Nor stoops to pity in the toad
The speechless sorrow of its eyes.

He asks no questions of the snake,
Nor plumbs the phosphorescent gloom
Where lidless fishes, broad awake,
Swim staring at a night-mare doom.

King Honour's Eldest Son

His father's steel, piercing the wholesome fruit
Of his mother's flesh, wrought acidly to mar
Its own Damascus, staining worse than war
A purity intense and absolute;
While her clean stock put forth a poisoned shoot,
In likeness of a twisted scimitar,
Sleek as a lovelock, ugly as a scar,
Wrong as the firstborn of a mandrake root.

There was a waning moon upon his brow,
A fallen star upon his pointed chin;
He mingled Ariel with Caliban;
But such a blossom upon such a bough
Convinced his poor progenitors of sin
In having made a something more than man.

Nonchalance

This cool and laughing mind, renewed
From covert sources like a spring's,
Is potent to translate the mood
Of all distraught and twisted things.

In this clear water shall be cast
Outrageous shapes of steel and gold,
And all their hot and clotted past
Beaded with bubbles silver-cold.

The moving power takes their heat
Into itself, forgetting them;
And warmth in trickles, slow and sweet
Comforts a fainting lily-stem.

South

Spotted by sun, and visible
Above me in a wave-green vault,
With that thick sticky linden-smell
Saturate, as the sea with salt.

Transmuting all the blue to green
And all the green to serpents' tongues,
Deep, ponderable, felt and seen,
And breathed in pain, with heavy lungs.

Is this that limber element
Which runs like light, and will not stop
To drink the apple's sap and scent
While thirsting for the mountain-top?

Demon Lovers

The peacock and the mocking-bird
Cry forever in her breast;
Public libraries have blurred
The pages of his palimpsest.

He wanders lonely as a cloud
In chevelure of curled perruque;
Masked assassins in a crowd
Strangle the uxorious duke.

Castilian facing Lucifer,
Juan does not remove his cap;
Unswaddled infantile to her
His soul lies kicking in her lap.

While she, transported by the wind,
Mercutio has clasped and kissed. . . .
Like quicksilver, her absent mind
Evades them both, and is not missed.

Fable

A knight lay dead in Senlac:
One white raven stood
Where his breast-bone showed a crack:
She dipped her beak in blood.

The old man's lean and carven head
Was severed under the chin:
The raven's beak was varnished red
Where the veins ran small and thin.

Empty sockets sucked the light
Where the great gold eyes had shone:
Oh, but the raven's eyes were bright
With fire she supped upon!

The old man's beard was ravelled up
In stiff and webby skeins:
From his broad skull's broken cup
The raven sipped his brains.

Insensate with that burning draught
Her feathers turned to flame:
Like a cruel silver shaft
Across the sun she came.

She flew straight into God's house;
She drank the virtuous air.
A knight lay dead: his gutted brows
Gaped hollow under his hair.

IV: BEAVER UP

Castilian

Velasquez took a pliant knife
And scraped his palette clean;
He said, "I lead a dog's own life
Painting a king and queen."

He cleaned his palette with oily rags
And oakum from Seville wharves;
"I am sick of painting painted hags
And bad ambiguous dwarves.

"The sky is silver, the clouds are pearl,
Their locks are looped with rain.
I will not paint Maria's girl
For all the money in Spain."

He washed his face in water cold,
His hands in turpentine;
He squeezed out colour like coins of gold
And colour like drops of wine.

Each colour lay like a little pool
On the polished cedar wood;
Clear and pale and ivory-cool
Or dark as solitude.

He burnt the rags in the fireplace
And leaned from the window high;
He said, "I like that gentleman's face
Who wears his cap awry."

This is the gentleman, there he stands,
Castilian, sombre-caped,
With arrogant eyes, and narrow hands
Miraculously shaped.

Sequence

I

This is the end of all, and yet I strive
To fight for nothing, having nothing kept
Of loveliness that saved myself alive
Before this killing distillation crept
Numbing my limbs, and stiffening my tongue
To clay, less vital than the salted thorn
Whereon a tyrant's banneret is hung
As scarecrow for a harvesting still-born:
And I am barren in a barren land,
But who so breaks me, I shall pierce his hand.

This much is true, that there were certain times,
Measured by minutes, with a blank between,
When our two courages could meet, and climb
Into the blue above the blowing green;
But now the lifted pasture is too high,
The shoal too deep, for such were noble graves;
In this unlighted kennel, where to die
Will not awaken hounds, nor anger slaves,
I shall advise me to prepare my couch;
Here it is dark; for more I may not vouch.

II

One of these men will find my skeleton;
To one it will be delicate and slim,
With stars for eyes, and portent of a sun
Rising between the ribs to frighten him;
Yet, being bold, he might embrace it soon
With quick insensate passion in the night,
And by the holy taper of the moon
Encouraged, and because its bones were light
As filagree of pearl, he might depart
Bearing my jangled heart-strings on his heart.

And he might bury it in sand or sod,
Stamping it down to circumvent the wolf,
And, being kind, commend it to his God,
Whose Mind was swimming somewhere in the gulf
Above his head; but if that other found
The rotten framework of his servitor,
He'd leave it lying on the cluttered ground
Between a bottle and an apple-core,
And go his way, in agony and sweat,
Because he could not pity nor forget.

III

For various questions which I shall not ask,
And various answers which I cannot hear,
I have contrived a substituted task
To prove my body is devoid of fear;
To prove my spirit's elemental blood
Is pure, courageous, and uniform,
I shall submerge my body in the mud,
I shall submit my spirit to the storm;
I shall bend down my bosom to the snake,
As to an infant for its father's sake.

I shall persist, I shall pursue my way
Believing that his cruelty was fine
As tempered steel for chastening of clay,
Impatient of corrosions that were mine;
He that despised me shall not be forgot;
He that disparaged me shall be my lord;
That was a flambeau, half-consumed and hot,
This was the running light along a sword;
And though I warmed my fingers at the one,
The other is my father and my son.

Little Sonnet

Let your loving bondwoman
Salute your lips if you prefer;
This is your courtesy to her.
Yet still remember how she ran
From her grave, and running, leapt
To catch the arrows of your hurt,
To stretch her body in dust and dirt,
Flinging a causey where you stepped.

Remember how, asleep or waking,
The shallow pillow of her breast
Shook and shook to your heart's shaking,
In pity whereof her heart was split;
Love her now; forget the rest;
She has herself forgotten it.

Pity Me

Pity the wolves who prowl unsleeping
   Guarding the pasture from a thief;
Pity the proud leopards weeping
   Tears of subtle grief.

Pity the savage panthers sheathing
   Sharp disdain in silken gloves;
Pity the golden lions breathing
   Fire upon their loves.

Pity the prickly star that frightens
   The Christ Child with its shattered spear;
Pity the midnight when it lightens;
   Pity me, my dear.

Unfinished Portrait

My love, you know that I have never used
That fluency of colour smooth and rich
Could cage you in enamel for the niche
Whose heart-shape holds you; I have been accused
Of gold and silver trickery, infused
With blood of meteors, and moonstones which
Are cold as eyeballs in a flooded ditch;
In no such goblin smithy are you bruised.

I do not glaze a lantern like a shell
Inset with stars, nor make you visible
Through jewelled arabesques which adhere to clothe
The outline of your soul; I am content
To leave you an uncaptured element;
Water, or light, or air that's stained by both.

Benvenuto's Valentine

Not for the child that wanders home
So wasted by barbaric kings,
So wearied by imperial Rome,
That he will clasp my apron-strings.

Not for the ghost that never is
And never will be known by me,
Whose heel is on the precipice
Before its print has left the sea.

And not for darling Harlequin
Spinning in stars of diamond shape;
Nor Hamlet exquisite and thin
As moonbeams in an inky cape.

Not for the legend latest-born
Of Chivalry and Virgin, whom
Roland has knighted with a horn,
And Richard with a sprig of broom.

Not even for the man who climbed
A thousand miles to thrust a torch
Among forgotten fagots, rimed
By winter in an iron porch.

But for the thought, that wrought and planned
Such intricate and crystal things,
My kiss is set upon your hand
As softly as a silver ring's.

Twelfth Night

It has always been King Herod that I feared;
   King Herod and his kinsmen, ever since. . . .
I do not like the colour of your beard;
   I think that you are wicked, and a prince.

I keep no stable . . . how your horses stamp! . . .
   If you are wise men, you will leave me soon;
I have been frightened by a thievish tramp
   Who counted bloody silver in the moon.

You get no lodging underneath these roofs,
   No, though you pay in frankincense and
     myrrh;
Your harness jangles with your horses' hooves;
   Be quiet; you will wake him if you stir.

This is no church for Zoroastrians,
   Nor resting-place for governors from Rome;
Oh, I have knowledge of your secret plans;
   Your faces are familiar; go home.

And you, young captain of the lion stare,
   Subdue your arrogance to this advice;
You should forbid your soldiery to swear,
   To spit at felons, and to play at dice.

You have perceived, above the chimney ledge,
  Hanging inverted by Saint David's harp,
His sword from heaven, with the double edge
  Which, for your service, is no longer sharp.

He sleeps, like some ingenuous shepherd boy
  Or carpenter's apprentice, but his slim
And wounded hands shall never more destroy
  Another giant; do not waken him.

The counterpane conceals the deeper wound
  Which lately I have washed with vinegar;
Now let this iron bar be importuned;
  I say you shall not speak to him of war.

V: PLUMES

Now that Your Eyes are Shut

Now that your eyes are shut
Not even a dusty butterfly may brush them;
My flickering knife has cut
Life from sonorous lion throats to hush them.

If pigeons croon too loud
Or lambs bleat proudly, they must come to
    slaughter,
And I command each cloud
To be precise in spilling silent water.

Let light forbear those lids;
I have forbidden the feathery ash to smutch them;
The spider thread that thrids
The gray-plumed grass has not my leave to touch
    them.

My casual ghost may slip,
Issuing tiptoe, from the pure inhuman;
The tissues of my lip
Will bruise your eyelids, while I am a woman.

Lilliputian

She hoards green cheeses
On a high moonlight shelf;
Her tea-kettle freezes;
The child is an elf.

Her shiny mind is peopled
By brisk goblins, but
Though castled and steepled
The place is Lilliput:

Where I lie bound by subtle
Spider-web and hair,
And the small feet scuttle,
And the gold eyes stare.

Parting Gift

I cannot give you the Metropolitan Tower;
I cannot give you heaven;
Nor the nine Visigoth crowns in the Cluny Museum;
Nor happiness, even.
But I can give you a very small purse
Made out of field-mouse skin,
With a painted picture of the universe
And seven blue tears therein.

I cannot give you the island of Capri;
I cannot give you beauty;
Nor bake you marvellous crusty cherry pies
With love and duty.
But I can give you a very little locket
Made out of wildcat hide:
Put it into your left-hand pocket
And never look inside.

Francie's Fingers

"Oh, Francie, sell me your fingers
And I will pay you well!"
Sweet flowed that voice, the singer's,
As gillyflowers smell.

"Your fingers are a witch's,
White as china clay,
Thin as willow switches
Pointed up to pray.

"For your dinted knuckles
And blue printed wrist
I'll give you my buckles
Of paste and amethyst."

"I will sell my fingers
If you will sell your tongue;
Your voice is a singer's
Whose veins run song.

"If apples sprang from heaven
Instead of from the ground,
Their juice could not even
Be sweet as that sound."

"Oh, sell your smallest finger!"
"Your voice is all I fancy!"
"No, no!" replied the singer.
"Oh, no, no!" cried Francie.

Beware!

To Baba, Playing a Nocturne by Chopin

Baba flourishes and dips,
Little gestures poise and gleam;
Now her shiny finger-tips
Strike the surface of the stream.

Now she plunges both her wrists
In the water blue as air,
Curdling into starry mists,
Diapered with light despair.

Deep above the drowning sands
Sorrow like a moon is drowned;
Baba, only dip your hands
In the surface of the sound.

Gifts at Meeting

From the Greek

Violets, sparsely
Budded, to wreathe
With sprigs of parsley;
A kid to seethe
In its own juices
Dilute with wine;
Sweetmeats from cruises
Transpontine;
A sapling, studded
With apricocks,
Cream, new-crudded,
Butter in crocks;
A barrel of tunny,
A barley bun;
Combs of honey
That smell like the sun:
Plaited withies
Piled with white grapes;
From Persian smithies
Smooth dagger-shapes;
Cups of lapis
And mirrors of bronze;
Springes, to trap us
Geese and swans;
A wild deer's haunches
And a lion's head;
Coral branches
Silver and red;

A pirate's earring
And a painted book,
I bring you, fearing
Your blackthorn crook.

To Aphrodite, with a Talisman

This graven charm, that leads a girl unkissed
From bridal-bed; that knows to draw a man
Far over-seas; carved out of amethyst,
Chased with fine gold; accept, O Cyprian!

See where it lies, translucent, beautiful:
Oh, take it for your very own! and see
How it is bound with violet-coloured wool,
Gift of a sorceress from Thessaly.

To a Blackbird Singing

Marcus Argentarius

Where the poisonous mistletoe
Over the oak her magic weaves,
Sing no more, O blackbird! go
To safer shade of silver leaves.

Sing, and set your little foot
On golden grape and silver vine:
The Wine-God loves your song: the fruit
Will cool your lovely throat with wine.

On a Singing Girl

Musa of the sea-blue eyes,
Silver nightingale, alone
In a little coffin lies:
A stone beneath a stone.

She, whose song we loved the best,
Is voiceless in a sudden night:
On your light limbs, O loveliest,
May the dust be light!

To Claudia Homonœa

My words were delicately breathed
As Syren notes: the Cyprian's head
Never shone out more golden-wreathed
Than mine: but now I lie here dead.

A chattering swallow, bright and wild,
Whom one man loved for all her years—
Having loved her even as a child:
I leave him nothing but his tears.

TRIVIAL BREATH

I

Dedication

When I was seven years old I had a primer:
The immaculate bosom of the mother-tongue
Flowed milkily in mercy to the young,
Dispensing balsam to the infant dreamer.
How delicately did the silver skimmer
Of natural love select the cream along
The honied surface of that stream of song!
That cup of pearls dissolving into dimmer!

That breast of twin benevolent moons! That
    conduit
Whose veins are threaded with pellucid truth!
Into the hungry coffin and beyond it
A single uncorrupted drop of youth
Must live in elegy upon my lips
When I and chaos shall have come to grips.

I would that my possessions were the proper
And polished coinage of the stars and suns;
But for the earth I give you farthing bronze,
And for the planets I return you copper.
Fumes fallen from your ceremonial supper
Made aromatic harmony which once
Refreshed my childhood: even now it runs
Between our skies, the lower and the upper.

Oh, who was I to be so bravely suckled
At the early wells of English undefiled,
And by your grace, whose sacred hand unbuckled
Extreme Castalia for a careless child?
Yet this I grant the creature of uncommon;
She is your vassal while she is a woman.

That creature is your vassal ever since:
Perceiving the device upon your standard
To be the sign her infancy had pondered,
Her spirit was impulsive to convince.
If her opinion perishes or wins;
Be her fidelity approved or slandered;
The event is set: the woman never wandered
In vile devotion to a lesser prince.

Profuse and fabulous appeared the page
On which your youngest lessons were emblazoned:
Enchantments that unlock a crystal cage;
An alphabet with astral fire seasoned;
These are the characters of that largesse
Which gives the lavish greater to the less.

For that her blood is valiant and noble
I thank the language at her leaping source;
At best essential heaven; at bitter worse
A witch's brew of strong fantastic trouble:
But for your courtesy my thanks are double,
Who, as a matter of munificent course,
Diverted waves of influential force
To shape for me a rainbow-coloured bubble,

An innocent bird, an iridescent music,
To be my own for all the rest of living.
Oh, this was nourishment and wine and physic!
This was a proud extravagance of giving!
And I have nothing to return in kind
Save the dull mortal homage of the mind.

"Desolation Is a Delicate Thing"

Sorrow lay upon my breast more heavily than
    winter clay
Lying ponderable upon the unmoving bosom of
    the dead;
Yet it was dissolved like a thin snowfall; it was
    softly withered away;
Presently like a single drop of dew it had
    trembled and fled.

This sorrow, which seemed heavier than a
    shovelful of loam,
Was gone like water, like a web of delicate frost;
It was silent and vanishing like smoke; it was
    scattered like foam;
Though my mind should desire to preserve it,
    nevertheless it is lost.

This sorrow was not like sorrow; it was shining
    and brief;
Even as I waked and was aware of its going, it
    was past and gone;
It was not earth; it was no more than a light leaf,
Or a snowflake in spring, which perishes upon
    stone.

This sorrow was small and vulnerable and
    short-lived;
It was neither earth nor stone; it was silver snow
Fallen from heaven, perhaps; it has not survived
An hour of the sun; it is sad it should be so.

This sorrow, which I believed a gravestone over
    my heart,
Is gone like a cloud; it eluded me as I woke;
Its crystal dust is suddenly broken and blown
    apart;
It was not my heart; it was this poor sorrow
    alone which broke.

Minotaur

Go study to disdain
The frail, the over-fine
Which tapers to a line
Knotted about the brain.

Unscrupulous to pinch
And polish down the thin
And fire-encasing skin:
Which pares away an inch

Of valuable soil
Whereon a god took root,
Diminishing a brute
With pumice and with oil.

Distrust the exquisite,
The sharpened silver nerve,
The lacquered, nacred curve
Wherein a moon is lit.

Aristocratic skulls
Rejected as inept
That innocency kept
'Twixt orbèd eyes of bulls.

Black lava-crusted coins
Bear heavy brow and limb,
The monstrous stamp of him
Who sprang from Taurine loins.

Gaze ever and at length
Upon the carven head,
Devouring it as bread
To thrive upon its strength.

The sword-deflecting scar
Indented and oblique
That stripes the savage cheek;
The throat made columnar

In copper, and up-raised
To such a trumpet shape
No clangour can escape,—
These only must be praised.

This only is the cure,
To clasp the creature fast;
The flesh survives at last
Because it is not pure.

From flesh refined to glass
A god goes desert-ward,
Astride a spotted pard,
Between an ox and ass.

Let innocence enchant
The flesh to fiercer grain
More fitted to retain
This burning visitant.

Confession of Faith

I lack the braver mind
That dares to find
The lover friend, and kind.

I fear him to the bone;
I lie alone
By the beloved one,

And, breathless for suspense,
Erect defense
Against love's violence

Whose silences portend
A bloody end
For lover never friend.

But, in default of faith,
In futile breath,
I dream no ill of Death.

Malediction Upon Myself

Now if the dull and thankless heart declare
That this fair city is no longer fair
Because the month has peopled it with shadows
And swept the quality to hills and meadows:
Yea, if it cry in its ingratitude
That holy beauty is no longer good
But that it is degraded and cast down
Because it treads the pavement of the town:
If it accept the rank ignoble rule
That beauty is no longer beautiful
Because it is not straitlaced and aloof
But sets its sandal on a London roof
And takes polluted Thames to be its mirror:
If the vile heart is guilty of this error
I here pronounce upon its inmost nerve
The malediction which it must deserve.
Loosen its strings: let it no longer be
The instrument of mortal ecstasy:
Empty its veins of rapture, and replace
The fine elixir with a foul and base
Till the true heaven never more descends
In delicate pulses to my finger ends,

Or flutters like a feather at my heel.
Bind blindness on my forehead: set a seal
On each of my two eyes which have forsworn
The light, and darken them with disks of horn.
Stop up my nostrils in default of breath
With graveyard powder and compacted death,
And stuff my mouth with ruin for a gag,
And break my ankles of a running stag:
Let the long legs of which I am so proud
Be bended, and the lifted throat be bowed:
Lower the arrogant pennon which I bear
Blown backward in the fringes of my hair
And let its silk be trampled to a skein
Of serpents knotted in corruptive pain:
Let these my words unwind the virtuous mesh
Which knits the spirit to the naughty flesh:
Let me dismember me in sacred wrath
And scatter me in pieces for a path
On which the step of that I have denied
Descends in silver to his proper bride.

King's Ransom

About the Emperor's thumb revolving,
Mouthed by Manchu's enamelled dragon;
Upon the damasked barge, dissolving
Within the deep Egyptian flagon;

Downcast before the swine by Circe;
Poised between double diamond prisms;
Clipped by the horseshoe nail that hearsay
Declares a cure for rheumatisms;

If the artificer be Vulcan
Or microscopical Cellini
To set an eyeball for a falcon
Or carve a button for a genie;

And whether cupped in gold or copper,
In frigid silver or the burly
Embrace of bronze; stained by the upper
Cloud colours, or profound sea-pearly;

Whether consuming or congealing
In fire or salt; O never shall you
Find an enchantment for concealing
This little moon's enormous value!

True Vine

There is a serpent in perfection tarnished,
The thin shell pierced, the purity grown fainter,
The virgin silver shield no longer burnished,
The pearly fruit with ruin for its centre.

The thing that sits expectant in our bosoms
Contriving heaven out of very little
Demands such delicate immaculate blossoms
As no malicious verity makes brittle.

This wild fastidious hope is quick to languish;
Its smooth diaphanous escape is swifter
Than the pack of truth; no mortal can distinguish
Its trace upon the durable hereafter.

Not so the obdurate and savage lovely
Whose roots are set profoundly upon trouble;
This flower grows so fiercely and so bravely
It does not even know that it is noble.

This is the vine to love, whose balsams flourish
Upon a living soil corrupt and faulty,
Whose leaves have drunk the skies, and stooped to
    nourish
The earth again with honey sweet and salty.

Speed the Parting—

I shall not sprinkle with dust
A creature so clearly lunar;
You must die—but of course you must—
And better later than sooner.
But if it should be in a year
That year itself must perish;
How dingy a thing is fear,
And sorrow, how dull to cherish!
And if it should be in a day
That day would be dark by evening,
But the morning might still be gay
And the noon have golden leavening.
And beauty's a moonlight grist
That comes to the mills of dying;
The silver grain may be missed
But there's no great good in crying.
Though luminous things are mould
They survive in a glance that crossed them,
And it's not very kind to scold
The empty air that has lost them.
The limpid blossom of youth
Turns into a poison berry;
Having perceived this truth
I shall not weep but be merry.
Therefore die when you please;
It's not very wise to worry;
I shall not shiver and freeze;
I shall not even be sorry.

Beautiful things are wild;
They are gone, and you go after;
Therefore I mean, my child,
To charm your going with laughter.
Love and pity are strong,
But wisdom is happily greater;
You will die, I suppose, before long.
Oh, worser sooner than later!

Innocent Landscape

Here is no peace, although the air has fainted,
    And footfalls die and are buried in deep grass,
And reverential trees are softly painted
    Like saints upon an oriel of glass.

The pattern of the atmosphere is spherical,
    A bubble in the silence of the sun,
Blown thinner by the very breath of miracle
    Around a core of loud confusion.

Here is no virtue; here is nothing blessèd
    Save this foredoomed suspension of the end;
Faith is the blossom, but the fruit is cursèd;
    Go hence, for it is useless to pretend.

Hospes Comesque Corporis

And if the heart may split the skin
Of this intrinsic chrysalis
To make the ephemeral ghost within
The fugitive it is:

If even the thinnest ravelling bind
Escape to the abandoned shell:
The heart must set the hollow mind
Replying like a bell.

Before division of the suns
Take shears to cut a second's thread,
The mind must tick ecstatic once
To prove that it is dead.

And the small soul's dissolving ghost
Must leave a heart-shape in the dust
Before it is inspired and lost
In God: I hope it must.

II

Miranda's Supper

Virginia, 1866

Between the solemn portico's
Column and column the lady goes;
Between the proud and painted stalks,
Plucked from Corinth, Miranda walks;
Pale, elegant, at point to vanish;
Her shoes are French, her shawl is Spanish;
Her silk in pure Manchurian rustles;
Three novices went blind at Brussels
To weave the enigma of her scarf;
Her lawns amazed the India Wharf
With webbed enchantment like a witch's
Before they flew in feather-stitches
To flounce her meanest petticoat.
A pair of cameos clasp her throat,
Wherein Psyche, pink and cream,
Slim-handed slants the candle-beam
On Cupid, swooning in carnelian;
Such trifles are antique Italian.

Miranda is a gentlewoman:
She met the invader as a Roman
Who scorns, above the screaming battle, a
Vercingetorix or Attila.
Fair-haired barbarian hordes disperse
Without the comment of a curse
From bitten lips like beads of coral;
She never made her anger oral.

She remained a marble memory
To the Cambridge Captain Amory.
She used him like a prince's legate,
But, oh, her eyes—her eyes were agate!
His mild and courteous Platonics
Shattered on flesh as firm as onyx;
She taught the boy to know his betters:
He saw the crown and heard the fetters.

Between the peony and rose,
Slim and sallow Miranda goes;
In light that's neither gold nor lunar,
This one later, and that one sooner;
Between the yellow and silver both,
Between the swallow and the moth,
Between the heavy walls of box.
Seven! Seven! cry all the clocks;
Five old clocks that chime in chorus,
One the gift of the Grand Duke Boris,
Malachite, with Peter in bronze
Setting his horse at the Persian guns;
The clock with a print of the Flying Castle;
The singing-bird clock that came from Basel;
Bonaparte's clock, with the bees worn shabby;
And the clock with the voice of an English abbey.
Five aristocrats, gilt and argent,
Wound at the word of a raw top sergeant;
Wound by the paw of a brutal sentry,
To toll the obsequies of gentry,
In that Palladian temple standing
Empty over Peacock's landing.

Between the box and the brier stalks
Pensively Miranda walks;
The mingled scene is cool and acrid;
Conventual evening is sacred.
Night invests its vistas slowly, as
Moonlight blooms on the magnolias
Whose cups contain the Holy Ghost;
Nothing is lost! Nothing is lost!
The evening is an ardent chapel,
A garden fenced with flowering apple;
Every flower enfolds a candle
Impregnate with the breath of sandal
And ambergris; a chamber arrased
With prayer, where peace lies unembarrassed;
Lies asleep, and does not move
Under the arching orchard grove.
Nothing is lost, nothing is murdered;
All is safe and softly ordered.
Miranda kneels upon the grass;
The ruffles of her taffetas
Crackle and speak; the sound is crisper
Than her voice subdued to whisper.
The evening's vault is a cathedral;
Kneel and pray; forget the Federal!
Forget the foul receding fever;
Peace is immaculate as ever,
And seven thousand lovely acres
Once more Miranda's and her Maker's;
Edens relinquished one by one.

Miranda rises and goes on
To where upon a wooded crest a
Temple dedicate to Vesta—
Roman-Greek, a little bastard,
Pillars not of stone, but plastered—
Lends a look Hellenic-Latin
To a lawn like sea-green satin;
A structure elegant and airy,
They call the thing a belvedere.
Why does Miranda stand and shiver?
Here is Phœbe, with her quiver
Furred by moss, and here's Apollo;
But the summer-house is hollow,
Hollow are the negroes' quarters,
And far away, across the parterres,
The mansion hangs on a hill's summit,
Hollowness resounding from it;
Streaming from it like a pennant;
Desolation is its tenant.
Harps and horns and windy whistles
Overflow the empty vessels.
Where are all the souls that filled them?
Who has killed them? Who has killed them?
For a moment's space the lady
Feels her pulse's beat unsteady,
Hammering and helter-skelter;
But her heart is safe in shelter,
Willow-vaulted, verdant-pastured,
Secure in silver mail envestured.

Miranda buckles on her courage.
Nevermore the beast shall forage,
Rooting with its bloody tushes
Among the rose and lilac bushes;
Trampling with devil-hooves of iron
The velvet gardens that environ,
Calm, austere, aloof, commanding,
The pillars and roofs of Peacock's Landing.

Miranda steps across the lawn
More precisely than a fawn
That shakes the dew from delicate ankles;
Nothing is wounded, nothing rankles,
Nothing is wicked, nothing whispers;
All is safe as a church at vespers,
On Christmas Eve, when the bells cry Nowell!
Miranda takes her garden trowel;
She stoops, she kneels, she digs in the ground.
What is the thing that her hands have found?
Is it horror, or beautiful?
Is it a mandrake, is it a skull?
Is it a crucifix, is it a pistol?
The thing is a cup of Chinese Bristol.
Pure in colour, correct in shape,
Bright as embroidered Canton crepe;
Mongol faces, demure and pale,
Small as Miranda's finger-nail;
Almond eyes, impertinent, tilted,
Flowers of April suavely melted;
This is a cup to hold infusions
Of caravan tea reserved for Russians

Or brewed for the throat of a thirsty Manchu;
This is a charming cup, I grant you;
Better by far than the willow patterns
That make a lady's soul a slattern's!
Behold Miranda now uncover,
With lingering gestures of a lover,
A grave that brims with twenty moons
Filling the bowls of the silver spoons.
Her mind grew duller, her mouth grew muter,
Each time she stirred her tea with pewter,
Or touched a knife with a black bone handle;
Now she is lighted like a candle.
She tastes the sugar and the spice in
Simple porridge served on Meissin;
Gros bleu de Sèvres, Italian faience,
Hold starvation in abeyance;
Poverty begins to shine,
The crust of bread is steeped in wine;
All the miracle of Cana
May be performed by painted china,
And even the portent of the mass
Imprisoned in a crystal glass.

Miranda wakens from the dead;
Soon her table shall be spread
With alchemy of Belfast looms;
Tapers shall enchant the rooms
And make them populous as once;
Power shall flow from every sconce;
Like Delphic tripods they shall burn.
All the Peacocks shall return

As the sea's uncounted pebbles;
All the gray and golden rebels,
Fallen down like stars, to spangle
Earth, upon the Bloody Angle;
The devout and ivory ladies,
Back from heaven, back from Hades,
Back from other earthier scenes,
Baltimore and New Orleans;
Back from exile, back from durance,
Home again to proud assurance.

Here, prepared within an upper
Chamber, is Miranda's supper.
Now partake; it is her body;
And the carven cup is bloody
Where her fingers drew it forth
From mortality of earth.
Every broken crust and crumb
Savours of your coming home,
And the berries she has gathered
By divinity are fathered.
Eat the bread she is adoring,
Drink the water she is pouring;

Now approach, both man and ghost;
Nothing is lost! Nothing is lost!

Peter and John

Twelve good friends
Walked under the leaves,
Binding the ends
Of the barley sheaves.

Peter and John
Lay down to sleep
Pillowed upon
A haymaker's heap.

John and Peter
Lay down to dream.
The air was sweeter
Than honey and cream.

Peter was bred
In the salty cold:
His hair was red
And his eyes were gold.

John had a mouth
Like a wing bent down:
His brow was smooth
And his eyes were brown.

Peter to slumber
Sank like a stone,
Of all their number
The bravest one.

John more slowly
Composed himself,
Young and holy
Among the Twelve.

John as he slept
Cried out in grief,
Turned and wept
On the golden leaf:

"Peter, Peter,
Stretch me your hand
Across the glitter
Of the harvest land!

"Peter, Peter,
Give me a sign!
This was a bitter
Dream of mine—

"Bitter as aloes
It parched my tongue.
Upon the gallows
My life was hung.

"Sharp it seemed
As a bloody sword.
Peter, I dreamed
I was Christ the Lord!"

Peter turned
To holy Saint John:
His body burned
In the falling sun.

In the falling sun
He burned like flame:
"John, Saint John,
I have dreamed the same!

"My bones were hung
On an elder tree;
Bells were rung
Over Galilee.

"A silver penny
Sealed each of my eyes.
Many and many
A cock crew thrice."

When Peter's word
Was spoken and done,
"Were you Christ the Lord
In your dream?" said John.

"No," said the other,
"That I was not.
I was our brother
Iscariot."

A Strange Story

When I died in Berners Street
I remember well
That I had lights at head and feet
And a passing bell.

But when I died in Houndsditch
There came to lay me out
A washerwoman and a witch;
The rats ran about.

When I died in Holborn
In an old house and tall
I know the tapestry was torn
And hanging from the wall.

When I died in Marylebone
I was saying my prayers;
There I died all alone
Up four flights of stairs.

But when I died near Lincoln's Inn
The small gold I had
Surrounded me with kith and kin;
I died stark mad.

When I died in Bloomsbury
In the bend of your arm,
At the end I died merry
And comforted and warm.

The Puritan's Ballad

My love came up from Barnegat,
  The sea was in his eyes;
He trod as softly as a cat
  And told me terrible lies.

His hair was yellow as new-cut pine
  In shavings curled and feathered;
I thought how silver it would shine
  By cruel winters weathered.

But he was in his twentieth year,
  This time I'm speaking of;
We were head over heels in love with fear
  And half a-feared of love.

His feet were used to treading a gale
  And balancing thereon;
His face was brown as a foreign sail
  Threadbare against the sun.

His arms were thick as hickory logs
  Whittled to little wrists;
Strong as the teeth of terrier dogs
  Were the fingers of his fists.

Within his arms I feared to sink
  Where lions shook their manes,
And dragons drawn in azure ink
  Leapt quickened by his veins.

Dreadful his strength and length of limb
   As the sea to foundering ships;
I dipped my hands in love for him
   No deeper than their tips.

But our palms were welded by a flame
   The moment we came to part,
And on his knuckles I read my name
   Enscrolled within a heart.

And something made our wills to bend
   As wild as trees blown over;
We were no longer friend and friend,
   But only lover and lover.

"In seven weeks or seventy years—
   God grant it may be sooner!—
I'll make a handkerchief for your tears
   From the sails of my captain's schooner.

"We'll wear our loves like wedding rings
   Long polished to our touch;
We shall be busy with other things
   And they cannot bother us much.

"When you are skimming the wrinkled cream
   And your ring clinks on the pan,
You'll say to yourself in a pensive dream,
   'How wonderful a man!'

"When I am slitting a fish's head
    And my ring clanks on the knife,
I'll say with thanks, as a prayer is said,
    'How beautiful a wife!'

"And I shall fold my decorous paws
    In velvet smooth and deep,
Like a kitten that covers up its claws
    To sleep and sleep and sleep.

"Like a little blue pigeon you shall bow
    Your bright alarming crest;
In the crook of my arm you'll lay your brow
    To rest and rest and rest."

Will he never come back from Barnegat
    With thunder in his eyes,
Treading as soft as a tiger cat,
    To tell me terrible lies?

The Devil in Seven Shires

A Carol for Midsummer Eve

Come all ye sorrowful people
Who would escape my fires;
Climb to the top of the steeple
And I'll show you seven shires.

The first is the shire of rivers;
The shire of a double dream
Whose image never shivers
In its mercurial stream.

The towers of Ys have hollowed
Tall caverns in the waves,
So this smooth stream has swallowed
A hundred hermits' caves,

A hundred wells of peace, no less,
And not a single town;
This is the shire for weariness;
Dive into this, and drown.

The second is the shire of iron
Where swords grow up like grain,
And granite walls environ
A broad resounding plain.

This radiant plain amazes
All men of noble will,
Where daggers grow like daisies;
Leap into this, and kill.

The third is the shire of apples
That are sweeter than holy bread;
I have torn down all the chapels
And builded inns instead;

Cider and beer in barrels;
And no man needs to think
Of war or money or quarrels;
Drop into this, and drink.

The fourth is the shire of sovereigns;
They cover the ground like leaves.
Thank God no justice governs
This heaven of my thieves!

They say the gold was given in alms
For Jesus Christ His sake,
But if any of you have itching palms
Steal into this, and take.

The fifth is the shire of whispers;
Its willow trees have tongues,
And soft infernal vespers
Ring bells between their songs;

And if you would betray your lord
Or see your brother die,
It needs, perhaps, but half a word;
Creep into this, and lie.

The sixth is the shire of shadows;
It shines within a cloud;
Silver are all its meadows;
Its birds sing low and loud;

Its clover valleys lie asleep
Forgetting to be sad;
If you would bury sorrow deep,
Go seek it, and go mad.

The seventh is the shire of pigeons
Queen Venus calls her doves,
Of Puck's and Pan's religions
And Ashtaroth her groves.

Ho! Young man with the missal-book,
What are you dreaming of?
Look in the bower below you, look!
Lean into this, and love.

"As I Went Down by Havre de Grace . . ."

As I went down by Havre de Grace
I saw the laurel in the wood:
The hours (I said) are sands that pass,
And some are bad and some are good;
Some are black and some are bright,
Yet all were darker, I suppose,
In lands where laurel is waxen white
And never white suffused with rose.

As I went up by Forty Fort
I saw the dogwood on the hills:
Life (I said) is hard and short
And riddled by a hundred ills:
Yet how much heavier I had gone,
How far from all my heart's desire,
In lands where dogwood never shone
Twisted by a tongue of fire.

As I went on by Steepletop
I saw wild strawberries underfoot:
Life (I said) is a water-drop
That falls upon a rotten root:
Yet were my grave the more profound
And planted thick with worser seeds,
Had I been nourished in a ground
Where strawberries never grow wild like
      weeds.

As I looked over by Isle au Haut
I saw the balsam in the grove:
Life (I said) is a flake of snow
That melts upon the bough above:
And I am murdered and undone,
But I was not bred in the middle land
Or in any valley under the sun
Where these dark trees disdain to stand.

As I went out by Prettymarsh
I saw the mayflower under the leaves:
Life (I said) is rough and harsh
And fretted by a hundred griefs:
Yet were it more than I could face,
Who have faced out a hundred dooms,
Had I been born in any place
Where this small flower never blooms.

The Innocents

When the cock in the dish
Crew "Christus natus est!"
I saddled a wish
And rode from the west.

The ditches were piled
With young children dying:
I saw Herod's child
In a gold cradle lying.

At high white noon
In a tower turned south;
A silver spoon
Was in the child's mouth.

It was bright as a candle
And heavy as lead:
Carved on the handle
Was John Baptist's head.

I climbed like a cat;
I stole the metal;
I hammered it flat
To a silver petal.

I curled the leaf
To a silver bell
To echo the grief
Of Israel.

The dead were dumb
But it spoke for them:
By night I was come
To Bethlehem.

Mary's mantle
Covered the Christ:
With myrrh and santal
His hair was spiced.

I kissed the ground
Where the gold was tossed:
The bell made a sound
Like a young child lost.

"This bell is a bird
Or a shaken bud;
It speaks a word
The colour of blood.

"This bell is a cup
Or a thorny cap . . ."
The Christ sat up
In Mary's lap.

"O take this bell
And stifle its breath,
For Israel
Is tired of death.

"When Herod's boy
  Lies broken and dying,
  Give him this toy
  To quiet his crying."

The Coast Guard's Cottage

Poor creature, come!
I should think shame to be afraid
Of what the waters and the winds have made
Flesh of a mortal man, lately my fellow:
Although the starving waves have stained you sallow
Or salty blue, indeed I shall not care,
Nor wonder at the seaweed in your hair,
Nor if your eyes be blind:
I swear I shall not mind
Such trifles, nor unkindly turn away
If I should find my shift dripping with spray.
Come, ghost, and lay
Your head upon my heart; you have come home.
Have cruel fishes made your kisses dumb?
You must not weep, my dear; 'tis bitter harm
They've done you, but the coverlid is warm,
And pity, softer than a feather bed,
Is comfortably spread
To soothe your body which the sea has broken;
Come, 'tis the truth I've spoken.
In this small cottage all the crying latches
Have told of you, and seawater in patches

Upon the stairs preserves the very print
Of your lost step; my pillows hold the dint
Of your cold, aching, and bewildered skull:
I'll never ask if you were beautiful
In life, or straight and slender:
Come, let me render,
As tenderly as my desires can
Peace to the shattered image of a man.
In this small cottage you and I alone
Move among wood and stone
And senseless things, and I alone am living,
Young, and unwounded; will you be forgiving
Of that unequal wrong
Which murdered you, and left me whole and strong?
It is some sad mistake;
Come, ghost, and take
The little warmth of my more vital limbs:
No creature flies or swims
Which can dismay my heart; you have come home.
I never was afraid of any ghost;
Dear love, you are not lost;
Nay, do not shiver; do not ever doubt.
Now blow the candle out;
Come to my bed;
I shall not be afraid.

III

Where, O, Where?

I need not die to go
So far you cannot know
My escape, my retreat,
And the prints of my feet
Written in blood or dew;
They shall be hid from you,
In fern-seed lost
Or the soft flakes of frost.
They will turn somewhere
Under water, over air,
To earth space or stellar,
Or the garret or cellar
Of the house next door;
You shall see me no more
Though each night I hide
In your bed, at your side.

Unwilling Admission

Here is the deep admission, whose profound
And difficult verity is out of reach
For loose adventure and impatient speech;
How, lying on your heart, I have not found
Treason nor failure in its mortal sound:
It is not necessary to beseech
A bodily vow to bind us each to each
Whose veins are rooted in heroic ground.

In such uncounted piercing of your side
Some river in heaven over-brimmed and broke,
And your least courage wore a lion's pride:
No several hammer of your pulses spoke,
Save to affirm, "The brave have never died,"
Though you and I must die at every stroke.

False Prophet

When I was forty, and two feathers sprung
Like crescents silver-curved from either temple,
Above a casque of bronze, I saw the simple
And casual shape of beauty; and my tongue
Spoke thus: "I am rejoiced I am not young
Lest this supreme and ultimate example
Of fine-spun flesh should very lightly trample
Upon my wounds; my withers are unwrung."

He might have been my son, save that my youth,
Bending the slender bow of its despair,
Loosed no such luminous arrow on the air;
His shaft was cut from some diviner bough:
And while my fainting heart perceived the truth,
My tongue spoke thus: "He cannot hurt me now."

A Red Carpet for Shelley

I

But this is nothing; an eccentric joke,
The legendary patchwork of a year
Flung into muddiness, like Raleigh's cloak,
To ask the honour of your step, my dear.
Your path is printed on the atmosphere
Forever as a flame against the smoke
Of obscure vision, and I must invoke
Your magnanimity to make it clear.

If I might spread soft words like living grass
Laid smooth beneath the heavy wheels of Time;
If I might loose the river of a rhyme
Or build a pavement out of gold and glass
Providing Heaven for you to walk upon,
It would be well; it would be better done.

II

The only engine which can fabricate
Language from spirit is the heart of each;
Industrious blood has braided into speech
The airy filaments of love and hate.
I have the labour of my own estate,
A pitiful machine which shall not reach
A single stellar thread; I cannot teach
Its narrow nerves the virtue to be great.

If my devout affection had been given
Commensurate power, which doubt nor custom
    dulls;
If I possessed the pure and fiery pulse
By true divinity informed and driven,
I would unroll the rounded moon and sun
And knit them up for you to walk upon.

III

The little sum of my experience
Remains the sole contrivance I produce
To weave this mesh, to colour and confuse
These ragged syllables with soul and sense.
I have been put to one supreme expense;
This was the noblest tincture I could use,
This the most subtle grain; I cannot choose
The dye to turn the lacklustre intense.

I have the proper scarlet of my veins,
The clean involved precision of my mind,
And you, who are so excellently kind,
Will not reject the tissue of my pains,
Stained by mortality's vermilion
To make a world for you to walk upon.

IV

Forgive the savage texture of the spoil
Tinted so barbarously by the clay
The rusty iron and the ocean-spray
Which lifted up my body from the soil.
Forgive the complicated brittle coil
Of my infirm invention, which I lay
Where you may pause, and pass, and never stay.
Here are the shocks of maize, the honey and oil,

The fruits like harvest moons, the fabulous land,
The crystal hills, the veiled prismatic plain;
And you will come, and you will not remain,
Nor leave a trace along the gilded sand.
So presently you will be come and gone;
Here's a strange road for you to walk upon.

Address to My Soul

My soul, be not disturbed
By planetary war;
Remain securely orbed
In this contracted star.

Fear not, pathetic flame;
Your sustenance is doubt:
Glassed in translucent dream
They cannot snuff you out.

Wear water, or a mask
Of unapparent cloud;
Be brave and never ask
A more defunctive shroud.

The universal points
Are shrunk into a flower;
Between its delicate joints
Chaos keeps no power.

The pure integral form,
Austere and silver-dark,
Is balanced on the storm
In its predestined arc.

Small as a sphere of rain
It slides along the groove
Whose path is furrowed plain
Among the suns that move.

The shapes of April buds
Outlive the phantom year:
Upon the void at odds
The dewdrop falls severe.

Five-petalled flame, be cold:
Be firm, dissolving star:
Accept the stricter mould
That makes you singular.

To a Book

By some peculiar force centrifugal
Snatched from my mind's protective keeping
Your path is plain and unequivocal,
A lightning-feathered falcon, leaping
To trace a hieroglyph in heaven.
O little moon! O lucent circle!
You are beyond my reach, and even
Beyond the fortune of a miracle.
A stubborn archangelic levity
Has whirled you into alien ether
But still a silver thread of gravity
Must bind our pulses up together.
In your beloved veins the earthy
Is mingled with the superhuman
Since you are mine, and I was worthy
To suckle you, as very woman.

The seedling of another planet
That holds our own in light derision
You clove the subterranean granite
To rainbows of the rock's division:
And like an aureate grain of mustard
Folding a golden microcosm
You fell between my breasts, which fostered
The shape of your sidereal blossom.

To a Book.

FACSIMILE OF A FAVORITE POEM OF ELINOR WYLIE'S,
IN HER OWN HANDWRITING

This poem, "To a Book," first appeared in "Trivial Breath."
It is the only complete poem surviving written in the poet's own hand

Now you are flown upon a power
Whose sovereignty is half-deceptive:
For you are free, my dragon-flower,
And still forever you are captive.
You shall remain a moon untarnished
By all contagion of our metal.
Yet this inferior substance furnished
The roots of that elusive petal:

A moon remaining pure and luminous,
So far removed, yet never further,
No prophecy, however ominous,
Pollutes with spiritual murther.
O smaller than a pearl's beginning
Within my brain! what living virtue
Informed your growth, and set you spinning
Where no malicious dust can hurt you?
Above terrestrial malfeasance,
Above the ignorant delusion,
With summer in successive seasons
To light you in divine transfusion
Of crystalline and opalescent,
No arrow of the world can startle
Your lunar quietude, my crescent:
Remember that your birth was mortal.

Last Supper

Now that the shutter of the dusk
    Begins to tremble in its groove,
I am constrained to strip the husk
    From everything I truly love.

So short a time remains to taste
    The ivory pulp, the seven pips,
My heart is happy without haste
    With revelation at its lips.

So calm a beauty shapes the core,
    So grave a blossom frames the stem,
In this last minute and no more
    My eyes alone shall eat of them.

Lament for Glasgerion

The lovely body of the dead,
Wherein he laid him down to rest,
Is shrunken to corruption's thread;
The blood which delicately dressed
The flying bone, the sighing breast,
One with nothingness is made.

The darling garment is outworn;
Its fabric nourishes the moth;
The silk wherein his soul was born,
Woven of flesh and spirit both,
Is crumpled to a pitiful cloth:
His soul lies naked and forlorn.

So one that walks within the air,
Who loves the ghost below the ground,
Rejoices fervently to wear
A body shaken and unsound;
A brow divided by a wound;
A throat encircled by a care.

Shall I go warm above the cold
Wherein he sleeps without a shroud
Or shred of beauty left to fold
About the poor soul's solitude?
The vanishing dust of my heart is proud
To watch me wither and grow old.

Tragic Dialogue

"Does not the progressive wheel of years
  Composed of baser metals
  Obscure him from your eyes, whose tears
  Have turned to willow petals?

"A hundred years! This iron bar
  Has beaten you, and hindered?"
"Not so: on no extremest star
  Had he and I been kindred.

"Ah no, both happily and alas!
  A clover field, a river,
  A hawthorn hedge, a pane of glass
  Had parted us forever."

ANGELS AND
EARTHLY CREATURES

I: ONE PERSON

Although these words are false, none shall prevail
To prove them in translation less than true
Or overthrow their dignity, or undo
The faith implicit in a fabulous tale;
The ashes of this error shall exhale
Essential verity, and two by two
Lovers devout and loyal shall renew
The legend, and refuse to let it fail.

Even the betrayer and the fond deceived,
Having put off the body of this death,
Shall testify with one remaining breath,
From sepulchres demand to be believed:
These words are true, although at intervals
The unfaithful clay contrive to make them false.

I

Now shall the long homesickness have an end
Upon your heart, which is a part of all
The past no human creature may recall
Save you, who are persuasive to unbend
The brows of death, and name him for a friend:
This ecstasy is supernatural;
I have survived to see the heavens fall
Into my hands, which on your hands depend.

Time has prepared us an enduring bed
Within the earth of this beloved land;
And, lying side by side and hand in hand,
We sleep coeval with the happy dead
Who are ourselves, a little earlier bound
To one another's bosom in the ground.

II

What other name had half expressed the whole
Of that incomparable and touching grace
Which spells the shape of danger in your face?
It is the very pattern of your soul;
The eagle's home, above the moon's control,
Above the seas, the high precipitate place;
The stairway cut from planetary space;
The crystal steps which climb a steeper goal.

The shadow of its light is only this:
That all your beauty is the work of wars
Between the upper and the nether stars;
Its symmetry is perfect and severe
Because the barbarous force of agonies
Broke it, and mended it, and made it clear.

III

"Children and dogs are subject to my power,"
You said, and smiled, and I beside you smiled,
Perceiving my unwisdom of a child,
My courage of a wolf new-taught to cower:
Upon the grass, beneath the falling flower,
I saw my spirit silent and beguiled
Standing at gaze; a brute no longer wild;
An infant wearied by the difficult hour.

And am I not your child who has come home?
And am I not your hound for faithfulness?
Put forth your hand, put forth your hand to bless
A creature stricken timorous and dumb,
Who now regards you with a lover's eyes
And knows that you are merciful and wise.

IV

Now am I Orson to your Valentine
Forever, and I choose it shall be so;
For how should the uncivil brier grow
Germane in nature to the noble vine?
The savage should be servant to the fine;
The falcon fly superior to the crow;
O dear my lord, believe me that I know
How far your virtues have outnumbered mine.

And you have levied final tribute now—
Your chivalry demanding the pretence—
You have constrained your vassal to avow
That we are equals, lest a violence
Be suffered by our love, and so I must
Deny the intrinsic difference in our dust.

V

The little beauty that I was allowed—
The lips new-cut and coloured by my sire,
The polished hair, the eyes' perceptive fire—
Has never been enough to make me proud:
For I have moved companioned by a cloud,
And lived indifferent to the blood's desire
Of temporal loveliness in vain attire:
My flesh was but a fresh-embroidered shroud.

Now do I grow indignant at the fate
Which made me so imperfect to compare
With your degree of noble and of fair;
Our elements are the farthest skies apart;
And I enjoin you, ere it is too late,
To stamp your superscription on my heart.

VI

I have believed that I prefer to live
Preoccupied by a Platonic mind;
I have believed me obdurate and blind
To those sharp ecstasies the pulses give:
The clever body five times sensitive
I never have discovered to be kind
As the poor soul, deceived and half-divined,
Whose hopes are water in a witch's sieve.

O now both soul and body are unfit
To apprehend this miracle, my lord!
Not all my senses, striving in accord
With my pure essence, are aware of it
Save as a power remote and exquisite,
Not seen or known, but fervently adored.

VII

Would I might make subliminal my flesh
And so contrive a gentle atmosphere
To comfort you because I am not there;
Or else incorporate and carve afresh
A lady, from the chilly heaven and clear
Which flows around you like a stream of air,
To warm and wind you in her body's mesh.

So would I cherish you a loving twice;
Once in a mist made matter; once again
In my true substance made ethereal:
And yet I cannot succour you at all
Whose letter cries, "My hands are cold as ice,"
The while I kiss the colder air in vain.

VIII

O love, how utterly am I bereaved
By Time, who sucks the honey of our days,
Sets sickle to our Aprils, and betrays
To killing winter all the sun achieved!
Our parted spirits are perplexed and grieved
Severed by cold, and change that never stays;
And what the clock, and what the season says
Is rumour neither valued nor believed.

Thus absence chills us to apparent death
And withers up our virtue, but together
We grow beyond vagaries of the weather
And make a summer of our mingled breath
Wherein we flourish, and forget to know
We must lie murdered by predestined snow.

IX

A subtle spirit has my path attended,
In likeness not a lion but a pard;
And when the arrows flew like hail, and hard,
He licked my wounds, and all my wounds were
    mended;
And happy I, who walked so well-defended,
With that translucid presence for a guard,
Under a sky reversed and evil-starred;
A woman by an archangel befriended.

Now must I end the knightly servitude
Which made him my preserver, and renounce
That heavenly aid forever and at once;
For it were neither courteous nor good
If we, who are but perishable things,
Should hang another weight between his wings.

X

When I perceive the sable of your hair
Silvered, and deep within those caverns are
Your eyesockets, a double-imaged star,
And your fine substance fretted down by care,
Then do I marvel that a woman dare
Prattle of mortal matters near and far
To one so wounded in demonic war
Against some prince of Sirius or Altair.

How is it possible that this hand of clay,
Though white as porcelain, can contrive a touch
So delicate it shall not hurt too much?
What voice can my invention find to say
So soft, precise, and scrupulous a word
You shall not take it for another sword?

XI

"Before I die, let me be happy here."
The glass of heaven was split, and by that token
I knew the bubble of my heart had broken;
The cool and chaste, the iridescent sphere,
Filled, in that vernal season of the year,
With sapling's blood, the beechen and the oaken
And the green willow's; when the word was spoken
This innocence did faint and disappear.

So have I lost my only wedding dower,
The veins of spring, enclosed within my heart,
Traced small in silver like a celestial chart;
And I am vanished in the leaf and flower,
Since, at your voice, my body's core and pith
Dissolves in air, and is destroyed forthwith.

XII

In our content, before the autumn came
To shower sallow droppings on the mould,
Sometimes you have permitted me to fold
Your grief in swaddling-bands, and smile to name
Yourself my infant, with an infant's claim
To utmost adoration as of old,
Suckled with kindness, fondled from the cold,
And loved beyond philosophy or shame.

I dreamt I was the mother of a son
Who had deserved a manger for a crib;
Torn from your body, furbished from your rib,
I am the daughter of your skeleton,
Born of your bitter and excessive pain:
I shall not dream you are my child again.

XIII

O mine is Psyche's heavy doom reversed
Who meet at noon, part by diminished light,
But never feel the subtle balm of night
Fall merciful upon a body pierced
By extreme love; and I considered first
That you, a god more prodigally bright
Than the lesser Eros, had enriched my sight,
Made your own morning, and the stars immersed.

But secondly I saw my soul arise
And, in the hushed obscure, presume to creep
Tiptoe upon your spirit laid asleep,
And slant the impious beam across your eyes;
And I believe I have my just deserts
Lacking the shadow of peace upon our hearts.

XIV

My fairer body and perfected spirit,
Beyond metempsychosis, and beyond
The faults you must forgive me to be fond,
Are yours in any death that I may merit;
Mortality has wearied us who wear it,
And they are wiser creatures who have shunned
This miry world, this slough of man's despond,
To fortify the skies we shall inherit.

I have entreated you to grant me Time
To memorize the pure appointed task;
Today it is Eternity I ask
In which to learn the lesson of this rhyme:
Its liberal periods are not too wide
To educate me fitly for your bride.

XV

My honoured lord, forgive the unruly tongue
That utters blasphemies; forgive the brain
Borne on a whirlwind of unhallowed pain:
Remember only the intrepid song;
The flag defended and the gauntlet flung;
The love that speech can never render plain;
The mind's resolve to turn and strive again;
The fortitude that has endured so long.

My cherished lord, in charity forgive
A starveling hope that may at times desire
To warm its frozen fingers at your fire;
'Tis by such trifles that your lovers live,
And so rise up, and in the starlight cold
Frighten the foxes from your loneliest fold.

XVI

I hereby swear that to uphold your house
I would lay my bones in quick destroying lime
Or turn my flesh to timber for all time;
Cut down my womanhood; lop off the boughs
Of that perpetual ecstasy that grows
From the heart's core; condemn it as a crime
If it be broader than a beam, or climb
Above the stature that your roof allows.

I am not the hearthstone nor the cornerstone
Within this noble fabric you have builded;
Not by my beauty was its cornice gilded;
Not on my courage were its arches thrown:
My lord, adjudge my strength, and set me where
I bear a little more than I can bear.

XVII

Upon your heart, which is the heart of all
My late discovered earth and early sky,
Give me the dearest privilege to die;
Your pity for the velvet of my pall;
Your patience for my grave's inviolate wall;
And for my passing bell, in passing by,
Your voice itself, diminished to a sigh
Above all other sounds made musical.

Meanwhile I swear to you I am content
To live without a sorrow to my name;
To live triumphant, and to die the same,
Upon the fringes of this continent,
This map of Paradise, this scrap of earth
Whereon you burn like flame upon a hearth.

XVIII

Let us leave talking of angelic hosts
Of nebulæ, and lunar hemispheres,
And what the days, and what the Uranian years
Shall offer us when you and I are ghosts;
Forget the festivals and pentecosts
Of metaphysics, and the lesser fears
Confound us, and seal up our eyes and ears
Like little rivers locked below the frosts.

And let us creep into the smallest room
That any hunted exile has desired
For him and for his love when he was tired;
And sleep oblivious of any doom
Which is beyond our reason to conceive;
And so forget to weep, forget to grieve,
And wake, and touch each other's hands, and turn
Upon a bed of juniper and fern.

II: ELEMENTS AND ANGELS

Love Song

Had I concealed my love
And you so loved me longer,
Since all the wise reprove
Confession of that hunger
In any human creature,
It had not been my nature.

I could not so insult
The beauty of that spirit
Who like a thunderbolt
Has broken me, or near it;
To love I have been candid,
Honest, and open-handed.

Although I love you well
And shall for ever love you,
I set that archangel
The depths of heaven above you;
And I shall lose you, keeping
His word, and no more weeping.

Chimæra Sleeping

Ah, lovely thing, I saw you lie
Within a beam of the sun's eye,
Where falling light and flying shade
Were bound together in a braid
Made of sky and earth colour:
Leaves blew over the forest floor:
The shadows were their noonday least.
I knew you neither man nor beast,
Nor god, nor rebel angel lost,
But that foreknown and holy ghost,
Beauty's pure pathetic shape;
The trap I never shall escape;
The heavenly bait; the honey breath
Issuing from the jaws of death.
So I approached, bereft of power,
And saw the pattern of a flower
Which moved in light and clearly shone
Under the arch of your breast-bone:
I saw a flower of white and green
Growing where your heart had been,
And grass obscured and dimly lit
As though a stream flowed over it:
Yea, through your body pale as glass
I saw the petals of the grass
Wave in the wind and softly stir

As seaweed under seawater.
You lay forlorn, hollow and thin
As a serpent's winter skin
From which his life of fiery gold
Has crawled away and left it cold:
And through your cold transparent flesh
The grass grew delicate and fresh;
I saw its blades, exact and plain
Through the blank crystal of your brain:
And nothing remained of fear and grief
Save the clear air and the green leaf;
And these the wind hath power to move;
And nothing there remained of love.
Then sorrow and joy dissolved my clay
To see you thus, and far away;
Your body laid upon the lawn;
Your spirit fled like a fox or fawn;
Your body consumed to silver ash
Whence passed the soul of the lightning flash;
Whence passed the lightning's living blood:
And I pursued you from the wood,
And, as I followed on, I wept
To leave the thicket where you slept.

Absent Thee From Felicity Awhile

"Spirits that walk beside me in the air—
Having laid by, in your impatience,
The bonds of body and sense—
Tell me how long I must forbear
The ecstasy of going hence
And still submit to wear
The mask of this pretence.

"Beloved creatures, who have left alone
Your sister in the ways you would not tread,
O excellent kind dead!
Have you forgot the burden of the bone?
The skull that clips my head
Is nowise lighter grown
Since your bright skins were shed."

Thus, upon middle earth, did I begin
My question, and the dead replied; "Submit:
Woman, who would be quit
Of this close panoply you walk within,
How ten times more unfit
Is his disguise, though worn threadbare and thin
By fire too fine for it!

"Consider who is your companion,
An hour obscured, but evident to our eyes,
Behind the slight disguise,
As light, and scarcely lesser than the sun;
Yet is he trapped within a skeleton
When even the transparent skies
Had clouded such an one.

"If you lament today, how must he faint
Between the ribs of stiff mortality?
Is it not plain to see
That heaven's own mind could not invent,
To clothe a river or a tree,
His soul's equivalent
Perfected in degree?

"O thank those stars, that even now are set
To grace the festival of your homecoming,
Like candles in a ring
About a board where friends are met,
That, upon earth, you found this subtle thing
Caught in the common net,
Beside you, wing to wing."

Felo De Se

My heart's delight, I must for love forget you;
I must put you from my heart, the better to please you;
I must make the power of the spirit set you
Beyond the power of the mind to seize you.

My dearest heart, in this last act of homage,
I must reject you; I must unlearn to love you;
I must make my eyes give up your adorable image
And from the inner chamber of my soul remove you.

Heart of my heart, the heart alone has courage
Thus to relinquish; it is yourself that stills you
In all my pulses, and dissolves the marriage
Of soul and soul, and at the heart's core kills you.

O Virtuous Light

A private madness has prevailed
Over the pure and valiant mind;
The instrument of reason failed
And the star-gazing eyes struck blind.

Sudden excess of light has wrought
Confusion in the secret place
Where the slow miracles of thought
Take shape through patience into grace.

Mysterious as steel and flint
The birth of this destructive spark
Whose inward growth has power to print
Strange suns upon the natural dark.

O break the walls of sense in half
And make the spirit fugitive!
This light begotten of itself
Is not a light by which to live!

The fire of farthing tallow dips
Dispels the menace of the skies
So it illuminate the lips
And enter the discerning eyes.

O virtuous light, if thou be man's
Or matter of the meteor stone,
Prevail against this radiance
Which is engendered of its own!

Hymn to Earth

Farewell, incomparable element,
Whence man arose, where he shall not return;
And hail, imperfect urn
Of his last ashes, and his firstborn fruit;
Farewell, the long pursuit,
And all the adventures of his discontent;
The voyages which sent
His heart averse from home:
Metal of clay, permit him that he come
To thy slow-burning fire as to a hearth;
Accept him as a particle of earth.

Fire, being divided from the other three,
It lives removed, or secret at the core;
Most subtle of the four,
When air flies not, nor water flows,
It disembodied goes,
Being light, elixir of the first decree,
More volatile than he;
With strength and power to pass
Through space, where never his least atom was:
He has no part in it, save as his eyes
Have drawn its emanation from the skies.

A wingless creature heavier than air,
He is rejected of its quintessence;
Coming and going hence,
In the twin minutes of his birth and death,
He may inhale as breath,
As breath relinquish heaven's atmosphere,
Yet in it have no share,
Nor can survive therein
Where its outer edge is filtered pure and thin:
It doth but lend its crystal to his lungs
For his early crying, and his final songs.

The element of water has denied
Its child; it is no more his element;
It never will relent;
Its silver harvests are more sparsely given
Than the rewards of heaven,
And he shall drink cold comfort at its side:
The water is too wide:
The seamew and the gull
Feather a nest made soft and pitiful
Upon its foam; he has not any part
In the long swell of sorrow at its heart.

Hail and farewell, beloved element,
Whence he departed, and his parent once;
See where thy spirit runs
Which for so long hath had the moon to wife;
Shall this support his life
Until the arches of the waves be bent
And grow shallow and spent?
Wisely it cast him forth
With his dead weight of burdens nothing worth,
Leaving him, for the universal years,
A little seawater to make his tears.

Hail, element of earth, receive thy own,
And cherish, at thy charitable breast,
This man, this mongrel beast:
He ploughs the sand, and, at his hardest need,
He sows himself for seed;
He ploughs the furrow, and in this lies down
Before the corn is grown;
Between the apple bloom
And the ripe apple is sufficient room
In time, and matter, to consume his love
And make him parcel of a cypress grove.

Receive him as thy lover for an hour
Who will not weary, by a longer stay,
The kind embrace of clay;
Even within thine arms he is dispersed
To nothing, as at first;
The air flings downward from its four-quartered
    tower
Him whom the flames devour;
At the full tide, at the flood,
The sea is mingled with his salty blood:
The traveller dust, although the dust be vile,
Sleeps as thy lover for a little while.

This Corruptible

The Body, long oppressed
And pierced, then prayed for rest
(Being but apprenticed to the other Powers);
And kneeling in that place
Implored the thrust of grace
Which makes the dust lie level with the flowers.

Then did that fellowship
Of three, the Body strip;
Beheld his wounds, and none among them mortal;
The Mind severe and cool;
The Heart still half a fool;
The fine-spun Soul, a beam of sun can startle.

These three, a thousand years
Had made adventurers
Amid all villainies the earth can offer,
Applied them to resolve
From the universal gulph
What pangs the poor material flesh may suffer.

"This is a pretty pass;
To hear the growing grass
Complain; the clay cry out to be translated;
Will not this grosser stuff
Receive reward enough
If stabled after labouring, and baited?"

Thus spoke the Mind in scorn:
The Heart, which had outworn
The Body, and was weary of its fashion,
Preferring to be dressed
In skin of bird or beast,
Replied more softly, in a feigned compassion.

"Anatomy most strange
Crying to chop and change;
Inferior copy of a higher image;
While I, the noble guest,
Sick of your second-best
Sigh for embroidered archangelic plumage:

"For shame, thou fustian cloak!"
And then the Spirit spoke;
Within the void it swung securely tethered
By strings composed of cloud;
It spoke both low and loud
Above a storm no lesser star had weathered.

"O lodging for the night!
O house of my delight!
O lovely hovel builded for my pleasure!
Dear tenement of clay
Endure another day
As coffin sweetly fitted to my measure.

"Take Heart, and call to Mind
Although we are unkind;
Although we steal your shelter, strength, and
  clothing;
'Tis you who shall escape
In some enchanting shape
Or be dissolved to elemental nothing.

"You, the unlucky slave,
Are the lily on the grave;
The wave that runs above the bones a-whitening;
You are the new-mown grass;
And the wheaten bread of the Mass;
And the fabric of the rain, and the lightning.

"If one of us elect
To leave the poor suspect
Imperfect bosom of the earth our parent;
And from the world avert
The Spirit or the Heart
Upon a further and essential errand;

"His chain he cannot slough
Nor cast his substance off;
He bears himself upon his flying shoulder;
The Heart, infirm and dull;
The Mind, in any skull;
Are captive still, and wearier and colder.

" 'Tis you who are the ghost,
Disintegrated, lost;
The burden shed; the dead who need not bear it;
O grain of God in power,
Endure another hour!
It is but for an hour," said the Spirit.

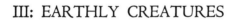

III: EARTHLY CREATURES

Fair Annet's Song

One thing comes and another thing goes:
Frosts in November drive away the rose;
Like a blowing ember the windflower blows
And drives away the snows.

It is sad to remember and sorrowful to pray:
Let us laugh and be merry, who have seen today
The last of the cherry and the first of the may;
And neither one will stay.

Robin Hood's Heart

The whole of him except his heart
Was lying straight and still,
And that was pulling his ribs apart
To climb to the top of a hill.

"Get up; get up; the sheets are clean;
The pillow is smooth and even;
Climb the hill, for we have not seen
One half our fill of heaven;

"One half our fill of heaven on earth
And the sun on the red deer's haunches;
The bridge between our death and birth
Is only a matter of inches.

"Throw off your laundered sheets and climb;
The grave is not forgiving,
And he who shortens his life in time
May lengthen it in living.

"If a little vein within me broke,
The blood would frighten your pillow;
But there's brave red earth beneath the oak
And water beneath the willow,

"That are not scared of any man's blood
When once he's left off breathing;
The rabbits frolicking in the wood
Will sniff and think it nothing.

"At the little noise our death will make
No red deer need stand still;
Get up; get up, for heaven's sake,
And climb to the top of the hill."

The Mountaineer's Ballad

It is not every gentleman
Who owns a rawhide lash
Will waste it on his bitches
And suchlike yellow trash.

The mountain laurel grows so high
To hide him from the earth;
The woods are full of creatures
That lie not by his hearth;

That lie not by his hearth to lick
His hand in gratitude;
There's plenty wolves and catamounts
Prowling in the wood.

It is not every gentleman
Will sit down in peace,
With his wife at his shoulder
And his children at his knees.

Perhaps, to be contrary,
He'll hang his rifle up,
And push away his supper,
And empty his cup.

And go out into the wild laurel,
Stepping tiptoe-tip,
Carrying nothing in his hand
But a rawhide whip.

O sometimes a gentleman
Will leave his rifle home
A-hanging in the firelight
While he goes forth to roam

In the darkness, on the mountain-side,
In a cavern of stars,
Thinking maybe of marriages,
And maybe of wars.

And maybe of the creature
That runs at his heel,
Clad in rough velvet
And shod with smooth steel;

That runs forever at his right hand
Like a sleek lightning-flash,
And he with nothing to defend him
But a rawhide lash.

Hughie at the Inn

Is it not fine to fling against loaded dice
Yet to win once or twice?
To bear a rusty sword without an edge
Yet wound the thief in the hedge?
To be unhorsed, and drown in horrid muck,
And in at the death, by luck?
To meet a masked assassin in a cape
And kill him, and escape?
To have the usurers all your fortune take,
And a bare living make
By industry, and your brow's personal sweat?
To be caught in the bird-net
Of a bad marriage; then to be trepanned
And stranded on foreign land?
To be cast into a prison damp and vile,
And break bars, with a blunt file?
To be cut down from gallows while you breathe
And live, by the skin of your teeth?
To defy the tyrant world, and at a pinch
To wrest from it an inch?
To engage the stars in combat, and therefrom
Pluck a hair's breadth of room?
Is it not fine, worthy of Titans or gods,
To challenge such heavy odds?
But no, but no, my lad;
'Tis cruel chance gone mad;
A stab in the back; a serpent in the breast;
And worst that murders best.

Such broad and open affronts to fear and pain
Breed maggots in the brain;
They are not valour, but the merest rash
Rubbish and balderdash.
Fortune's a drab, and vice her native soil,
And the button's off her foil.
Season your ale, now these long nights draw in,
With thought to save your skin:
Be provident, and pray for cowardice
And the loaded pair of dice.

Nonsense Rhyme

Whatever's good or bad or both
Is surely better than the none;
There's grace in either love or loathe;
Sunlight, or freckles on the sun.

The worst and best are both inclined
To snap like vixens at the truth;
But, O, beware the middle mind
That purrs and never shows a tooth!

Beware the smooth ambiguous smile
That never pulls the lips apart;
Salt of pure and pepper of vile
Must season the extremer heart.

A pinch of fair, a pinch of foul.
And bad and good make best of all;
Beware the moderated soul
That climbs no fractional inch to fall.

Reason's a rabbit in a hutch,
And ecstasy's a were-wolf ghost;
But, O, beware the nothing-much
And welcome madness and the most!

Bread Alone

Let not the heart's intention
To be both brave and good
Cheat that devoted engine
Of spiritual food.

Because it is not cruel,
Because it is not great,
Provide it fire, and fuel
Sufficient for its state.

Ah, poor machine, and faithful,
That limps without a wing!
My love, be never wrathful
With this imperfect thing.

To a Cough in the Street at Midnight

God rest you if you're dead;
And bless, and send you safely home to bed
If you are only old:
God cure your cold,
Whether it be but a cold in the head
Or the more bitter cold which binds the dead.

Farewell, Sweet Dust

Now I have lost you, I must scatter
All of you on the air henceforth;
Not that to me it can ever matter
But it's only fair to the rest of earth.

Now especially, when it is winter
And the sun's not half so bright as he was,
Who wouldn't be glad to find a splinter
That once was you, in the frozen grass?

Snowflakes, too, will be softer feathered,
Clouds, perhaps, will be whiter plumed;
Rain, whose brilliance you caught and gathered,
Purer silver have reassumed.

Farewell, sweet dust; I was never a miser:
Once, for a minute, I made you mine:
Now you are gone, I am none the wiser
But the leaves of the willow are bright as wine.

IV: ELEGIES AND EPISTLES

The Broken Man

Dear love, when I was seven and a half,
I dreamed this prologue to your epitaph,
Precise in miniature, and more exact
In fantasy than the mechanic fact:
I adored your double in a china figure,
Or you, a shadow that the sun makes bigger.
I loved this prodigy better than myself;
He lived upon a lady's mantel-shelf;
His eyes were gold; his hair a sable silvered:
My heart beheld him, borrowed, begged, and pilfered,
Until the lady, with a look oblique,
Said, "Darling, you may take him if you like;
I have found a most enchanting pair, of Chelsea."
Then, like an aspen, in ecstatic palsy,
From head to foot I shook with happiness:
The thing was you, and neither more nor less
Than my true love, whom I have always known
Whether shaped of air, or alabaster stone,
Or earth, or fire; your own true self it was,
Whom later I translated into glass
To make a mockery of the thing adored:
It was a little image of my lord;
Or else presentiment caused the counterfeit
Presentment to appear as exquisite
Almost—for I must only say "almost"—
As the child of Mary and the Holy Ghost.
I dreamed my china creature was divine;
I was his mother; he was safely mine;
He was my lover, waited and welcome:
Through feathered snow I tiptoed to my home.

Thus was inaugurate the ordeal of pain
That made you iron, who were porcelain:
Ah, poor anatomy, the type and token
Of mortal love, how often were you broken!
Poor love, compounded out of clay and sand,
How often were you broken in my hand!
Alas the child, that had the will to cherish,
And you were broken, and at point to perish!
Yet were you never quite completely killed,
Or ground to powder, and your beauty spilled;
You were too fine for me, and far too good,
Who had deserved a stick of hickory wood;
And you were battle-scarred and tempest-tossed,
And rescued late; miraculously lost,
Abandoned, and beneath an attic rafter,
Lifted from drifted dust a fortnight after;
And (most yourself) you suffered all the while
Without a word, and with a little smile:
My father said: "You've smashed your china boy."
And put you coolly, like a common toy,
In that green bag, which, as the grave our griefs,
Garnered the scanty harvest of his briefs.
O, had my father truly been your friend,
Dear love, it had been kinder in the end
To sweep you to a heap of china clay,
And smooth your bed, and leave you where you lay
In rainbow bits, and all your troubles ended!
He took you to a shop and had you mended:
And, through the porcelain white as buds of privet,
A clever artisan had thrust a rivet,
Until, from silver head to scarlet heel,
You were become a gentleman of steel

Which pierced your vitals to preserve you whole,
The iron even entering your soul,
Which, by this brutal pang, contrived to save
The pieces of the bravest of the brave:
So, in this cruel fashion, were you mended;
And you were broken; but you were not bended.
And then, as now, most intricately knit
From iron and its earthen opposite,
From clay's fragility and its crumbling petal,
And from the nobler fabric of the metal,
The stuff of fields, the substance of the sword,
I recognized the image of my lord,
Whom I have loved, whom I have ever known
Whether in light or in the thunder-stone;
The broken man, who broke my heart in half
In this strange prologue to your epitaph.

The Lie

A fortnight past you looked at me and lied:
Then my heart fainted, and I thought it died.
But O, that engine's not so simply stilled
Burns you for fuel, so I was not killed!
It was the moment, not myself, was slain,
And faith grew crescent in the mind again.
Then did I seek, according to my use,
Your full, sufficient, and extreme excuse
For having varied, by a hair's breadth span,
From your true character of god in man.
Through the dispersing vertigo of trance
I fixed my eyes upon your countenance,
Which is, to me, the elemental stuff
Of beauty perfected, and the mask put off;
And, in the deeps and colours of your eyes,
I saw the inverted images of lies
I tell you daily; yea, I saw them all,
Careless, case-hardened, and habitual.
Preposterous falsehoods, legendary oaths,
Transparent and disprovable untruths,
And idle tales at which an infant smiles,
And histories far-fetched a million miles.
To blame you for a fault were insolence
Upon my part, who multiply by tens
The initial crime that I condemn you for,
And, in an hour, contrive you twenty more.
For, while my soul protested and cried hush,
Have I not sworn to you without a blush
When I was ill, that I was very well?
That I was blessed, when most miserable?

And, while my teeth have chattered in my head
With cold, and sick desire to be dead,
Have I not checked my shivering and sworn
I lay in damask leaves without a thorn?
Have I not vowed, before I starved and swooned,
That you were ointment to my every wound,
And food and physic, and a crumb too much?
And have I not declared you such and such
And this and that, and all the tale untrue?
And have I never said I trusted you
Around the corner, world without an end,
To remain my lover and my loving friend?
Your constancy the stars', and not the moon's:
And I would trust you with my silver spoons!
O then, my darling, how have you deserved
The least reproach for having lightly swerved
By a width of spider's web, a honey bee's
Hair's breadth, or thread of silken eyelashes,
From the iron line of strict veracity,
And, by my faith, from such a liar as I?

The Loving Cup

The instrument of your reason being tuned
To the pitch of madness and desire to wound,
You would not drink my health save from her glass
Who drinks my death: can such things come to pass?
But I considered, striving to be just
(Who strive not to be loving, for I must),
That we, your vassals bound by every oath,
Are thus your vessels, and you drink from both:
That she and I, being each of us a woman,
Taste the elixir of your lips in common;
Though I alone am privy to the fact;
I have your half, and lesser than exact:
That I, having sworn I would devote my powers
To advance her interests as well as yours,
Am therefore chattel of yourself and her
And so divided into share and share.
Should I not count me more unfortunate
If from two cups you drank my single fate,
Than now, when both of you set lips to one
And from its sole brim drink division?
For you have drunk me joy and she despair
In the same wine, that served you share and share,
But never share and share alike: the mood
In which you drank transformed the wine to blood.
Although your mood was black, it did distill
Such essences as could not wish me ill;
While she, who smiled to drink my mortal pain,
Brewed hell itself within her smallest vein.
O, if from different cups you drank a curse,
Though yours was gold, and hers was something worse,

I were indeed undone! But you have blessed
Your own particular drop, and damn the rest!
Yet it is saved: your drop converts it all,
And makes it holy and medicinal:
She drinks her health (who drank to me disease),
Long life, and happiness and more than these;
Moons in solution; flavours of the sun's:
The cup is loving, having kissed you once.

To a Lady's Countenance

This unphilosophic sight;
This silly mask of silken white;
This thing which has, to hide its grief,
Less than a rose's lesser leaf;
This web a spider might have spun
With patience and precision;
This veil concealing sorrow's face,
Arranged with coquetry and grace,
Which shall remain, when all is said,
After sorrow itself is dead;
In colour, a camellia flower;
In shape, a whim of the glass-blower;
The mind's eye hollowed and made blind,
But not the brow above the mind;
And, whatsoever may be starved,
The little lips uncut, uncarved;
God's power has disdained to mould
This clay so delicate and cold;
Perchance he took it for the flesh
Of mushrooms, or the silkworm's mesh;
Stuff too slight to bear the fine
Finger-tip of the divine
In lines of noble heritage;
And so, you do not show your age.

Little Elegy

Withouten you
No rose can grow;
No leaf be green
If never seen
Your sweetest face;
No bird have grace
Or power to sing;
Or anything
Be kind, or fair,
And you nowhere.

HITHERTO
UNCOLLECTED POEMS

The Bird

O clear and musical,
Sing again! Sing again!
Hear the rain fall
Through the long night.
Bring me your song again,
O dear delight!

O dear and comforting,
Mine again! Mine again!
Hear the rain sing
And the dark rejoice!
Shine like a spark again,
O clearest voice!

Green Hair

I know you wonder why I wear
The hat which I have called Green Hair
And why I cover up my own
Which has a tawny chestnut tone
Warm, when all its lights are lit,
As a swarm of bees with the sun on it.
You say bronze hair is prettier
Than this strange green of feathery fur;
But there's a charm in this strange green
Which is so nearly blue; I've seen
A comb of coral set with pearls
Drawn through lengths of such green curls
In the green gloom of a chilly cave
Down, far down in a hollow wave;
And under ancient forest trees
Long green tresses such as these
Shadow like a falling veil
Shy secret faces, dusky pale;
And I have seen green locks like those
Deep in a glacier, under snows.
I have seen such green hair tossed
From the brows of a creature wandering lost
On the other side of a waning moon,
And in the golden sun at noon
I have seen young April plait
Flowers in showery hair like that,
And wring the rain from it in drops,
And spread it to dry on green hill-tops.

Now do you wonder that I wear
The hat which I have called Green Hair?
Thus with witchcraft I am crowned
And wrapped in marvels round and round;
There's sorcery in it, and surprise;
Believe your own dark-amber eyes
When mine of hazel look at you
Turned to incredible turquoise blue.

Pretty Words

Poets make pets of pretty, docile words:
I love smooth words, like gold-enamelled fish
Which circle slowly with a silken swish,
And tender ones, like downy-feathered birds:
Words shy and dappled, deep-eyed deer in herds,
Come to my hand, and playful if I wish,
Or purring softly at a silver dish,
Blue Persian kittens, fed on cream and curds.

I love bright words, words up and singing early;
Words that are luminous in the dark, and sing;
Warm lazy words, white cattle under trees;
I love words opalescent, cool, and pearly,
Like midsummer moths, and honied words like bees,
Gilded and sticky, with a little sting.

Nameless Song

My heart is cold and weather-worn,
　A musical and hollow shell:
The winds have blown it like a horn,
　The waves have rung it like a bell.

The waves have whirled it round and round,
　The winds have worn it thin and fine:
It is alive with a singing sound:
　Whose Voice is that?　It is not mine.

Prayers from the Greek

TO ARTEMIS OF THE OAKWOOD, WITH A STATUE
(Mnasalcas)

This is your image, brightest of huntresses:
Shadow for the hunter all this oakwood's bounds,
Where you go afoot, over hills tossing with trees,
Hurrying, with terrible and eager hounds.

THE LOVER
(Callimachus)

May sleep so lie upon your breast
As I lie sleeping in the rain,
And as you gave your lover rest
May love give rest to you again.

The very passers-by are kind;
They succour him who sorrows most;
But never even in dreams your mind
Has dreamt of pity or her ghost.

O cruel, cruel! you do not care
Though I lie sleeping in the cold:
Perhaps the silver on your hair
May speak of this when you are old.

From a photograph by Nicholas Muray

TO THE SHEPHERD-GOD
(Theocritus)

Daphnis, the country pipe-player,
Offers these to Pan with prayer:
His river-reed that's pierced for singing;
The crooked stick he kept for flinging
At hares: his javelin sharp and slender:
His fawn-skin tawny-gray and tender,
Whose fur the faintest pattern dapples:
His little scrip that smells of apples.

Romance

The years' dark valleys
I have slipped between
To a park with alleys
Of close-clipped green

Here's a marble Love weathered
By sunlight and rain;
Like a dove blue-feathered
Shines a lady's bright train.

A flower, ashes
Stirred to flame, springs;
A shower flashes,
And a bird sings.

Dorimène, dreaming,
Listens, looks down;
Like rain streaming
Glistens her gown.

Hands white and waxen,
Each nail stained rose;
Hair bright and flaxen
Under pale snows.

Silver clings the powder
To her blond hair.
The bird sings louder
By the pond there.

The roses glow yellow,
And the skies are pearl;
Jacotot, poor fellow!
Sighs for this girl

Who spurns her lover
And her flowered age
As she turns over
A tear-showered page.

"Ah! le beau roman
D'Epiaxe! Hélas!
Le grand Cyrus son amant!
Tout passe! Tout lasse!"

Alas! so pass heroes!
Proud Love lies dead!
And above, Eros
Cries with bowed head.

Sleeping Beauty

Imprisoned in the marble block
  Lies Beauty; granite is her dress;
The strong may carve from living rock
  A lady like a lioness.

With hammer blow and chisel cut
  They make the angry Beauty leap.
For me the obdurate stone is shut;
  How shall I wake her from her sleep?

An acorn tossed against an oak,
  A hazel wand that turns—and look!
She parts the leaves, a pearly smoke,
  She cleaves the earth—a silver brook.

Shepherd's Holiday

Too honest for a gypsy, too lazy for a farmer,
What should you be but a shepherd on the hills,
Herding sheep with sad faces
Over grass-grown places,
High above a web of streams and willow-trees and mills?

Too tame for a gypsy, too wild for a dairy-maid,
What could I be but a silly goose-girl,
Tending hissing white snakes
By weed-green lakes,
Crying in the dew-fall with my hair out of curl?

Too silent for the neighbours, too simple for the towns-
    people,
What shall we do who love each other so?
I'll teach your gray sheep
To guard you from the steep,
You'll catch me back from drowning where my dark lake
    lies deep,
I'll pluck a feather pillow that shall sing you to sleep
Up among the rocks where the blueberries grow.

Thunder Storm

O for all soundless Time's
Deep spells to lock it!
O for a little chime's
Clear bells to mock it!

O for a calm, to smooth
Your senses by it!
O for a balm, to soothe
Your breast to quiet!

O for the power to call
Your peace, and breathe it!
O for an hour to fall
Asleep, beneath it!

O for your hand, to hush
Loud caves of thunder!
O for the burning bush,
And graves thereunder!

Priest. XXth Dynasty

Dive through thin black dust, and swim
Sniffing darkness thick with spices
Stiffened in the throat of him
Whose oblique enchantment ices
Man alive in mind and limb.

Old Mortality's cold plunge
Laps your living throat and muzzle,
Saps the strength with which you lunge
Choking in this joke or puzzle
His ambiguous bones expunge.

Bones expunge and bones expound
Dust's equivocal composure;
Lithe and slippery life is drowned,
Stifled in an eyelid's closure,
Sealed in lips without a sound.

The Persian Kitten

Lie still, my love, and do not speak, because
In silence is fulfilling of these laws;
Fastidious sorcery lives not in speech.
Let each devoutly take the hand of each,
But lightly, and without the emphasis
Of pressure, or persuasion of a kiss.

Breathe now with breath diminished to the least;
Narrow your eyelids to entreat the beast;
Make soft your glances; never show surprise
Discovering the lion in his eyes—
The little lion like a burning bush—

Approaching languidly, with *hush* and *hush*
Sighed from the padding velvet, see him crouch
And spurn the carpet for the painted couch,
Like a gilt feather on its pillows tossed.

Lie still, my love, lie still, or all is lost.

From violence of lust remote, withdrawn,
He shudders delicately to a yawn,
And with their pulses in a mute accord
Lies down between these lovers like a sword.

All Souls

It is God's honour on my head
That drives me forth to walk alone,
Among the lighter-footed dead,
Upon this hollow path of stone.

It is God's honour on my hands
That makes them cold in such a wise
That I must clench them; his commands
Thus mercifully stigmatize.

It is God's honour on my feet
That sets a nail in either shoe
To spur them down the common street;
This is the thing I always knew.

Unfinished Ballad

You stared at me and you never spoke;
My cool heart broke like a bubble;
You held a dagger beneath your cloak
So thin you could bend it double.

Your eyes were empty of any life,
But still you were smiling, smiling;
And your smile was nicked like the edge of your knife
And curled like an iron filing.

A little batswing on either foot
Was horror, and helter-skelter
I sweated and ran, who had learned to put
My head on your breast for shelter.

Three strong men stood up on a hill
At the rim of the first day's cycle;
I thought that the third was God until
The other two called him Michael.

Feathers of sky veiled every arm;
I hurried to half-believe him
When Michael shouted "He means no harm!"
And the other two cried "Forgive him!"

The soles of my feet were stayed in space;
I looked back over my shoulder;
And the devil himself had covered your face
With silver, or something colder.

The second day had a golden tinge;
Its dawn was a door to enter
Through a vision of palms in a wavy fringe
To red-hot sand in the centre.

A lion slept in a stripe of shade,
With his head bowed down on his bosom;
The locks of his mane were roughed and rayed
Like the leaves of a tawny blossom.

From bread of flesh and water of blood,
With innocent eyes of wonder,
He rose; his voice was a river in flood,
Its echo an arch of thunder.

Like the green sea racing the jungle ran
To break on the palm-tree hedges,
And the hunched gorilla that hates a man
Leapt out from the jungle's edges.

Prince of the powers of the air,
He dropped from deep dominions;
His shoulder-blades were plumed with hair
As an angel's are with pinions.

He stretched the leather between his lungs;
He beat with his fist for hammer;
The vines were heavy with spotted tongues
That stiffened and shook to clamour.

The indolent lion spoke at length;
"Can this spider-web image hurt you?
This ramshackle atomy lacking strength
And brave commensurate virtue?

"Many and many a time I've starved
On bones that were surely bigger
Than this poor filagree flayed and carved
To the shape of a human figure.

"The stuff of his spirit escapes my scorn;
He is nothing and less than nothing;
I could make of his body my drinking-horn
But I turn from that thirst with loathing.

"Listen! The knots of his sinews crack;
Look! How his thews are meagre;
But you have ridden astride my back
And laid to my breast a leaguer.

"Not by a smile and a rotten rib
Shall a daughter of mine be frightened,
For you have slept in my stony crib
And the strings of your heart are tightened."

Viennese Waltz

We are so tired, and perhaps tomorrow
Will never come; be fugitive awhile
From tears, and let the dancing drink your sorrow
As it has drunk the colour of your smile.

Your face is like a mournful pearl, my darling;
Go, set a rose of rouge upon its white,
And stop your ears against the tiger-snarling
Where lightning stripes the thunder of the night.

Now falling, falling, feather after feather,
The music spreads a softness on the ground;
Now for an instant we are held together
Hidden within a swinging mist of sound.

Forget these frustrate and unhappy lovers;
Forget that he is sad and she is pale;
Come, let us dream the little death that hovers
Pensive as heaven in a cloudy veil.

The Heart's Desire

Anger that is not anger, but bubbles and stars of colour, blood in the brain beating the nerves into a frenzy of inner light, magnified moons and suns swimming in the secret understanding that is more the body than the mind, the soul upon the lips for no reason at all, or at the sound of a door or the tinkle of gold and silver money in the street, faces best known and most remembered estranged and a million miles away, and strange greasy faces passing in the dust of evening and now returning illuminated into godhead, cruelty where it cannot be, kindness where hatred is as inevitable as the white rising of a morning where morning may after all never more rise, disintegrate yet exquisite destruction of the heart at the moment of waking, desire for death like the vagueness of a thirst for thin extravagant wine, unredeemed by fear, mortal and importunate screams of why, why, why, in the extreme desolation of regained consciousness, loneliness, loneliness and indolence that is forever stigmatized by itself as a spiritual inertia, but which is in reality the desperate desire for common sleep among the sounds of a camp or village in which kinsfolk are gathered together for protection against wolves or robbers out of northern immensities of snow, sudden and intolerable perceptions, clear and pitiless, which tear the rags from all cradles, marriage beds and death beds, dead persons wherever lying, and all graves and altars of the dead, the sword twisted, twisted and turned in the breast unceasingly at the recurrent thought of that cruelty which cannot be true, the throat full of tears to be drunk again augmented by bitterness and thirst, the enormous loneliness of the room floating like a glass tank full of horror over the eyes and the breast and the crossed hands and feet of the stone image upon the bed, the window of the mirror which looks out into nothing, the other windows which look out into earthquakes and the fall of Herculaneum, the beat of the heart against the breast-bone and the ribs, in the temples and in the finger-tips, the pillow for weariness, the comfort and the coolness, lost and grown synonymous with that cruelty which cannot be true, the golden head for which the dead heart cries, the dead heart turning, which so turned among falling towers, burning, burning and crying to the sky, the thing no longer recognizable cast up by a sea full of green ice, the birds which appear to weep for it, but are in reality making ready to devour it, wheeling and crying to each other in cruelty, in ecstasy, which is nevertheless forgivable because it is a hunger of the body and not a spiritual exaltation, the cruelty, that other cruelty, the blow turning blue over the heart, the sudden sliding drop into another half-sleep which is immediately startled to madness by the sound of the falling towers of Herculaneum and Troy, the smoke, the dust, the stench, which is better than the green ice and the snow untracked save by wolves whose tracks are red, the couch in the desert, the grave in the desert, the couch upon the mountainside, the grave under the stars, the rock which will not speak and the water which will not listen, falling, falling down the mountainside over the rock with a noise of voices, the recurrent blow over the heart, the blow over the heart and the bruise turning blue upon the flesh, the arms lifted up to a sky full of screaming birds and stars which are falling, falling over the mountainside upon the towers which house the golden head and the dead heart and the tongues of inextinguishable fire.

The Madwoman's Miracle

"Dig up, dig up your daughter's bones
That sleep on Highgate hill,
And tell me if the sapphire stones
Enrich her fingers still.

"Drag up, drag up your little boy's head
That in the grave lies down;
Say does his brow, these five years dead,
Preserve its golden crown?"

Thus spoke the witch to the madwoman,
Who, mournful as an owl,
Wondered to see Aldebaran
Shine through the witch's cowl.

In strong enchantment she uprose
Made docile by a spell,
To dig the earth till it disclose
The bottom of its well.

And all the while she wept, because
Tears were this woman's words,
Until her stained and wounded claws
Scratched on the coffin-boards.

She wept prefiguring a face
No longer beautiful,
But fretted into paper-lace
About a brittle skull.

She wept imagining a hand
No more a living thing,
But frayed into a ravelled band
Around a silver ring.

She cried on Mary, mother and saint . . .
For in the grave were laid
Two dolls immaculate with paint
And glossy with brocade.

On one a tinsel crown there was
Shaped into seven points,
The other wore rings of azure glass
To fit her finger-joints.

The execrations of the witch
Flew whistling over the farms;
The woman crouched beside the ditch
With her children in her arms.

Peregrine's Sunday Song

When I have grown foolish
And ripe for my grave,
O, I'll be a mulish
And stubborn old knave!

I'll open my coffer
That's gilt and engraved;
Only those who suffer
Shall share what I've saved.

I'll build a great castle
In the heart of the town,
Like a long golden tassel
The clouds have let down.

I'll spread a broad table
Where thieves may repair;
There'll be oats in my stable
For the murderer's mare.

Most brightly on one day
My lamp shall be lit,
And Sunday, Sunday,
Is the sad name of it.

For then to the churches
The gentlefolk come,
But the sinner searches
Bare streets for a crumb;

O, bare but for sparrows,
And these eating dung!
On his breast-bone his sorrows
Like mill-stones are hung.

The saved and the shriven
Have consecrate meat,
But the poor unforgiven
Get nothing to eat.

While bells from the steeple
Rain silver on grief,
I'll call wicked people
To pudding and beef.

To plum-cake and liquor,
To sugary buns;
O, I shall call quicker
The wickeder ones!

If my hand should be hostile
To these hungry friends
I'll climb fire and frost till
My pilgrimage ends.

If I held me their better
By the very least part
Of a hair, 'twere a fetter
That rusted my heart.

O, few merry-makers
Will come to my board;
No salt in the shakers
I'll need to afford.

Much weeping will season
The viands with salt,
But I'll give none a reason
To grieve for his fault.

Eve shall not eat apples
Nor Cain wheaten bread
While something yet dapples
His white hand with red.

His thanks none shall owe me
Save for courtesy's sake;
I'll let the young Salome
Cut slices of cake,

Which she'll bring on a platter
To everyone,
For why should it matter
To me about John?

None shall be so rude as
To show pity or pride;
Broken-necked Judas
Shall sit by my side.

My tables and trestles
May fall down accursed,
But I'll have filled vessels
To charity first.

"How got you this jam?" ask
The prudenter sort;
"This silver and damask?
This pastry and port?"

"By murder? By arson?
By stabbing a knight?
By strangling a parson?"
Perhaps they are right.

Now I sing this fasting
By an elder tree;
Life everlasting
Is not for me.

I've leave to squander
What I never can keep,
However I wander
Or walk in my sleep.

Doomsday

The end of everything approaches;
I hear it coming
Loud as the wheels of painted coaches
On turnpikes drumming;
Loud as the pomp of plumy hearses,
Or pennoned charges;
Loud as when every oar reverses
Venetian barges;
Loud as the caves of covered bridges
Fulfilled with rumble
Of hooves; and loud as cloudy ridges
When glaciers tumble;
Like creeping thunder this continues
Diffused and distant,
Loud in our ears and in our sinews,
Insane, insistent;
Loud as a lion scorning carrion
Further and further;
Loud as the ultimate loud clarion
Or the first murther.

Three Folk Songs

GRACE BEFORE MEAT

From the Gaelic

No man should be tempted
 To be greedy, and grumble
At the cup that he's emptied.
 Its meaning was humble;
Being only to offer
 A drink when he thirsted,
Yet the poor thing might suffer
 A death when he cursed it.

And that woman's ungrateful
 Who fails to encourage
A love like a plateful
 Of butter and porridge.
It cannot be venison
 Because she is angry;
Lacking its benison
 She'll live to go hungry.

Sure, the child in the cradle
 Has no call to be reckless,
Though his spoon is a ladle
 Of silver, and speckless.
Pride has but narrow bones;
 Maybe the pretty
Will end on his marrow bones
 Begging for pity.

Suppose, when you're lonely,
   There's naught in your kettles
But bread broken stonily
   And serpentish victuals.
Kneel down and be decent,
   Give grace to your Sovereign,
That your lives may be seasoned
   With honey and saffron.

LOVE SONG

From the Icelandic

I was a sea-gull flying north
In the wrong season's
Distress; some fear had cast me forth
And some malfeasance.
The wind conveyed me past control;
My plumes were slanted;
To dash myself against the Pole
Was all I wanted.
My brain was frozen in my head,
My iris blinded;
To be destroyed and quickly dead
Was all I minded;
To dash my body on the ice
In shining splinters
And pile it with a century's
Contiguous winters.
I saw a lighthouse looking out
Over the mirror
Of polished darkness; all my doubt
And aching terror
Importuned me to end my pain
Upon its turning,
To be no more than a bloody stain
And feathers burning.
A flinty arrow cleaving glass
My flight was certain;
It fell away like waves; it was
A woven curtain.

It closed behind me hard as stone,
A little chamber
Whose walls I battered all alone.
Translucent amber
That cages flies; a drowsy pool
That drowns a swimmer;
A cup of mandragore; a cool
And sheeted glimmer
Upon the eyelids asking death
To give them silence,
Possess no power submerging breath
Like that lost island's.
So while a heart may hammer once
I fled and circled,
Then flew into a setting sun's
Twilight that sparkled.
My wings caressed your hand, it seemed,
And folding, kissed it,
But since the business was dreamed
I can't untwist it.

LAMENT

From the Breton

The apple boughs bend down with fruit;
    The wall is far too old to mend;
The rout rides up in full pursuit;
    Never ask the end.

The princes send ambassadors
    And high catastrophes portend;
Their galleys drive on desolate shores;
    Never ask the end.

The Pope has tendered me a ring;
    The King of France will stand my friend;
The Devil has shown me a marvellous thing;
    Never ask the end.

William, lend me your hunting knife!
    This house is hollow to defend.
My fathers led a dolorous life;
    Never ask the end.

Cold Summer

Twilight is blue for seven weeks
Upon its borders, and beyond
Pure darkness splits to dagger-peaks
Of flawed and shivered diamond.

Between slim hills the atmosphere
Swims cold as wine in silver jugs;
The summers live minute and clear,
Coloured like Persian praying-rugs.

She whirls above this circumscribed
And patterned carpet, with a pair
Of tame attendant pigeons, bribed
By corn as yellow as her hair.

Enchanter's Handmaiden

Sir, it was not commanding me to climb
The glassy hill, or wring the bloody shirt;
Such tasks are done in seven years' weary time,
And the performer takes no mortal hurt.

(O, but it was giving me a netful of eels to turn into
    venison pasty!)

It was not asking me to hold the brand
White from the smithy, or receive the lash
Across my weeping; these to burn the hand
And brow with different sort of lightning flash.

(No, but it was leaving me a stableful of straw
    to spin into golden mittens!)

It was not even nailing down my wrists
And ankles to a wheel in cruciform;
I know your mills require many grists,
And each but grinds subsistence for the worm.

(O, but it was making me suckle an imp after
    promising he was a Christian!)

A Courtesy

Having conceived that this delight alone
Must be the corner stone
For all my building; having stripped it bare
Of you and found it fair;
Having accepted deprivation;
I have knelt down to bow
My brow upon the brow
Of granite; I have filled my empty hand
With running pulse of sand,
And twined my fingers in a bough of leaves;
I have pushed back my sleeves
To let the water twist
Its coolness round my wrist,
And I have kissed the comfortable moss
For cushioning a cross
Of racking timber sharp as childbirth bed;
I have embraced instead
Of love, a ponderable cloud of rain.

Let us return again
Together; let us kneel upon the grass
In quiet clear as glass,
Bending stiff necks and crooking stubborn knees
In courteous obsequies
For that poor wolf, but late mistitled Pride;
Let us be thankful that this beast has died,
And thankful for the silence of the trees,
As I was thankful for the cheer I had
To hear their chattering when I was sad.

Lavish Kindness

Indulgent giants burned to crisp
The oak-trees of a dozen shires
Adorning thus a will-o'-the-wisp
With momentary pomp of fires.

The waters of an inland sea
Were magicked to a mountain peak
Enabling dwindled pools to be
Cool to a single swallow's beak.

But whether prodigies of waste,
Or idle, or beneficent,
Such deeds are not performed in haste
And none has fathomed their intent.

Golden Bough

These lovely groves of fountain-trees that shake
A burning spray against autumnal cool
Descend again in molten drops to make
The rutted path a river and a pool.

They rise in silence, fall in quietude,
Lie still as looking-glass to every sense
Save where their lion-colour in the wood
Roars to miraculous heat and turbulence.

Portrait in Black Paint, With a Very Sparing Use of Whitewash

"She gives herself;" there's a poetic thought;
She gives you comfort sturdy as a reed;
She gives you fifty things you might have bought,
And half a hundred that you'll never need;
She gives you friendship, but it's such a bother
You'd fancy influenza from another.

She'd give the shirt from off her back, except that
She doesn't wear a shirt, and most men do;
And often and most bitterly she's wept that
A starving tramp can't eat a silver shoe,
Or some poor beggar, slightly alcoholic,
Enjoy with Donne a metaphysical frolic.

She gives away her darling secret hope
At dinner tables between eight and nine,
And she would give Saint Peter's to the Pope,
And coals to men of Newcastle-on-Tyne,
She would arrange a match for Solomon
Or give Casanova an adoptive son.

She does not give advice; that I admit;
Here's her sole virtue, and I'll count it double,
Forgiving her some crime because of it,
But she gives tiresome and endless trouble.
If you need rest, she'll straight contrive a racket;
If gaiety, she'll fetch a padded jacket.

And she gives love of the least useful kind
At which advanced civilization mocks;
Half, a Platonic passion of the mind,
And half, a mad desire to mend the socks;
She's always wishing to turn back the page
And live with children in a golden age.

She gives a false impression that she's pretty
Because she has a soft, deceptive skin
Saved from her childhood; yet it seems a pity
That she should be as vain of this as sin;
Her mind might bloom, she might reform the world
In those lost hours while her hair is curled.

She gives a vague impression that she's lazy,
But when she writes she grows intense and thorough;
Gone quietly and ecstatically crazy
Among the sea-blue hills of Peterboro;
She'll work within her cool, conventual flat
As self-sufficient as a Persian cat.

And she can live on aspirin and Scotch
Or British ginger beer and bread and butter,
And like them both, and neither very much;
And in her infancy she possessed a stutter
Which gives a strong impression that she's shy
When heard today, and this is verity.

But when she clothes herself in gold and silver
In the evening, she gives herself away;
Having remained a high, laborious delver
For all the hours of a sunny day,
At night she gives you rather the idea
Of mad Ophelia tutored by Medea.

She gives you nothing worth consideration;
The effervescence of enthusiasm
Is trivial stuff; she'll give you adoration
If you belong to her peculiar schism;
As, that a certain English man of letters
Need never call the Trinity his betters.

Sometimes she gives her heart; sometimes instead
Her tongue's sharp side. Her will is quick to soften.
She has no strength of purpose in her head
And she gives up entirely too often;
Her manners mingle in disastrous ways
"The Lower Depths" and the Court of Louis Seize.

Doubtless, she gives her enemies the creeps
And all her friends a vast amount of worry;
She's given oblivion only when she sleeps;
She says she loves the grave; but she'd be sorry
To die, while it is vanity to live;
"She gives herself;" what has she left to give?

She'd give her eyes—but both her eyes are blind—
And her right hand—but both her hands are
     weak—
To be "Careless to win, unskilled to find,
And quick—and quick—to lose what all men
     seek."
But whether this has truly been her story
She'll never know, this side of purgatory.

For a Good Girl

(For D. P.)

Two tasks confront King Honour's daughter
Whom the unlearned malign insult;
One clear and luminous as water,
The other stiff and difficult.

Pity is laid upon the noble
So plain an obligation
Its fair performance is no trouble;
The puzzle's in the other one.

To be recognizant of merit
Peculiar to yourself; to be
Chivalric to your stronger spirit
Which gives the weak impunity.

This is the mental arabesque you
Must constantly contrive within
Or how shall you survive to rescue
The little wicked from their sin?

For a Good Boy

(For G. P. Y.)

If I ransacked the moon for you, my lord,
Till images ungermane to our clay
And rhymes fantastic, delicate and gay
Involved you neatly in a silver cord,
You'd set inverted commas round the word
Of my extreme invention, and display
A lively mockery to scare away
All sorrow save the ultimate absurd.

But you've a magic of a nobler kind
Which makes frivolity intense and clear
As crystal, sharp with spiritual grace;
It is the natural temper of your mind
To laugh, and you will always laugh at fear
Because he wears so ludicrous a face.

Greek Chorus in Venetian Glass

Made for a Very Light Opera

HE

I awake from a cold dream
To a golden glimmer,
As from a winter stream
A frozen swimmer
Is cast upon banks of honey-flowers and thyme.

SHE

There's a mutter of fear in this cave
And a flutter of wonder,
As the quicksilver fringe of a wave
Is broken to delicate thunder;
And what is the heart of its word?
I am lost; I am near it.

HE

There's a flame in this place
That frightens my pulses,
And the same grace
That a wild sea-gull's is;
And for this thanks, and the sunny sound of
    this rhyme.

There's a tower of fire in the air,
And snowflakes falling;
Whence is the sound, and where?
And who is calling?
Is it a ghost? Is it a spirit? Is it a bird?

CHORUS

There's no luck born
In either bosom;
They will pluck the thorn
And crumple the blossom;
But now they are singing, and the sad thing is
    unheard.

A Tear for Cressid

All virtuous persons who hear this song
Whose lives are chaste and placid,
Let them stop their ears to the monstrous wrong
Was wrought long since by Cressid:
Let the good go down to their marble vaults
With wreaths of memory dressèd;
But all ye poor lovers who ever were false
Come shed a tear for Cressid.

Let the pure and noble go hand in hand
To the service of God addressèd;
But ye whose hearts are as shifting sand
Speak but a word for Cressid:
Let bridal pairs in their arrased halls
Lie in honour and pride embracèd;
But all ye fond lovers who ever were false
Come drink to the health of Cressid.

Now lift your voices, ye virtuous maids,
And walk in the sun enlacèd
To a virginal melody sung and played
To curse the sin of Cressid;
Then sweeten your souls with a carol that calls
The name of Mary blessèd;
But all ye fair ladies who ever were false
Come breathe a prayer for Cressid.

Come all ye sorrowful and forsworn,
Ye fallen and disgracèd,
With crosses woven of willow and thorn
To the resting-place of Cressid:
The roseleaf falls at intervals
Upon the grave unblessèd;
And let all true lovers who ever were false
Shed but one tear for Cressid.

Dark Mirror

The earth is untroubled
And purely designed;
Its beauty is doubled
By a noble mind.

The wonder and homage
Of such is a pool
Wherein a true image
Hangs cleanly and cool.

So washed and immersèd
The trees and the grass
Float in crystal, reversèd
As in a clear glass.

But alas for the mirror
Of a wicked brain
Where the shape of error
Hangs staring and plain!

In the mind of the wicked
The earth is not good;
The trees are naked,
And the seas are blood.

Close your eyes, bind them
With a white kerchief;
Cover them, blind them
With a broad green leaf.

Or turn them sunward
To dazzle them blind,
But never look downward
Through a wicked mind.

Little Eclogue

Poor Loneliness and lovely Solitude
Were sisters who inhabited a wood;
And one was fair as cressets in the skies,
The other freckle-faced, and full of sighs.
And Solitude had builded them a bower
Set round with bergamot and gillyflower;
Wide windows, and a door without a latch,
Below the brier and the woodbine thatch.
They lived like birds, on rustic crusts and crumbs,
Mushrooms, and blackberries, and honey-combs,
Cream in a bowl and butter in a crock;
The moon for lantern, and the sun for clock.
Decorum did simplicity enrich;
A Parian Diana in a niche
Over the windows, and a harp between
With strings like gilded rain against the green;
Trifles their parents, Austerity and Peace,
Had bought in Paris, or picked up in Greece.
An infant's skull, which Loneliness had found
Without the churchyard, in unhallowed ground,
Under a little cross of blackthorn sticks;
For Solitude an ivory crucifix
Carved in a dream perversely Byzantine;
A silver mirror of a chaste design,
And Plato in white vellum; in levant
Shelley and Donne, presented by her aunt
(Who might have been a Muse, had she been got
By Jupiter, but unluckily was not.)
And Solitude was grave and beautiful
As the evening star, but Loneliness was dull;

And one was wild and holy, one was tame;
About their appointed tasks they went and came
One like a moth, the other like a mouse.
Like a new pin the cool and ordered house;
For lightly its divided burden fell;
But one did worse, the other very well.
For whatsoever Solitude had touched
Was clean, and not a finger of her smutched;
But oft the milk had soured in the pan
To see poor Loneliness morose and wan;
And when she polished copper she became
Listless as smoke against the augmented flame;
And when she walked below the lucent sun
Her freckled face was dust, her hair was dun;
And still with meek affection she pursued
Her lovelier twin, her sister Solitude,
Who, while that she was pitiful and kind,
Preferred the forest, and her private mind.
One day this nymph escaped into the dawn
And fled away, contemptuous as a fawn;
And through the hours she ran like fire and steel;
Imagination followed her at heel;
And what delights she tasted as she roved
Are metaphysical, and remain unproved.
Then Loneliness fell to weeping like a fool;
And wandered forth, because the wind was cool,
To dry her tears beneath a bracken fan;
And found a sleeping demigod or man;
And gazed entranced upon the creature's face,
Which was adorable and commonplace.
And when she saw him laid upon the leaves
Her hair was silver-gold as barley sheaves;

And when she saw his eyelids folded thin
Her eyes were amber, and with stars therein;
And when she saw his eyelashes unclose
Her freckles were the dew upon a rose;
Yea, all her freckles melted with her heart
To sun and dew, which drew his lids apart
As though the sun were shining in his eyes;
And she was fair as cressets in the skies;
And when she left the shadow of the wood
She was far lovelier than Solitude.
Let you believe, let me unsurely guess
This wonder wrought upon poor Loneliness;
But what was done, to what intrinsic end,
And whether by a brother or a friend,
And whether by a lover or a foe,
Let men inquire, and gods obscurely know.

Indentured

I will not enter any cloud
And close its quiet on my mind,
And I must never be too proud
And always be too kind.

I must send my heart to a hard school
And educate it to be brave,
For it is wise to be a fool
And noble to be a slave.

Although enchanting caverns pierce
Beneath the crystal of the seas,
Beyond the stellar universe,
I will not enter these.

It is my duty, my desire,
And my irrevocable fate
To gather kindling for a fire
And scrub a common plate.

The virtuous and beloved dead
Need neither cassia buds nor myrrh,
But living men require bread
However they may err.

And if a cup is set before
A man who will not drink from it,
Why, there are other wines to pour
And fires to be lit.

To feed the beggar and the prince,
To warm the madman and the thief;
I have known this labour ever since
My mind accepted grief.

But I shall be more blessed than damned
When this my servitude is done,
And I have found the dark, and slammed
Its door against the sun.

Ejaculation

In this short interval to tear
The living words from dying air,
To pull them to me, quick and brave
As swordfish from a silver wave,
To drag them dripping, cold and salt
To suffocation in this vault
The which a lid of vapour shuts,
To shake them down like hazel-nuts
Or golden acorns from an oak
Whose twigs are flame above the smoke,
To snatch them suddenly from dust
Like apples flavoured with the frost
Of mountain valleys marble-cupped,
To leap to them and interrupt
Their flight that cleaves the atmosphere
As white and arrowy troops of deer
Divide the forest,—make my words
Like feathers torn from living birds!

Prisoner's Song

Now sunlight stained by rain
Falls delicately down,
And I am free, and far again
From the bird-lime of the town.

Still am I snared in air
And bound by strings of sand,
Who never yet was caught in a net
Spread by a mortal hand.

Mary at the Fair
or Advice from a Gypsy

The ring's no more than parcel-gilt;
Folly to pretend it!
The cup is cracked, the milk is spilt;
Crying will not mend it;
Here's a pill you cannot sweeten;
Here's a frosted cake you've eaten;
A penny, and you've spent it.

Though they tie you to a cart
And whip you through the city,
He who never gave his heart
Will never give his pity;
Dry your tears; admit your error;
Kiss your mouth within the mirror;
Thank your stars you're pretty.

Mary, you have made your bed
Out of briars and withies;
No one lies where you are laid
For a score of prithees;
Pillow stuffed with stinging nettles
Harsh as adamantine metals
From the devil's smithies!

Mary, wait another year;
Turn your mattress over;
You shall see it change, my dear,
To a field of clover:
When the first hour of April opens—
Look, my lass, I'll lay you tuppence—
You shall find a lover.

An American in England

Here Is a Marvel, and No God May Ban It.
An Olive Branch, Grown in New England Granite.

I love every stock and stone
Of this land, no more my own;
Which we lost, that it might be
Wider by half a world of sea;
We cleft the rock with bitter toil
Having left our roots in sweeter soil,
Or torn them up and bid them thrive
Like mandrakes, bloody but alive:
Dust and sweat were wholesome salves
Until our hearts were cut in halves.
Ah, that was a prodigious wound;
A severing of sacred ground;
That was bad; but this is best;
Let the uprooted mandrake rest.
Love the good and leave the fault;
Sow not his several graves with salt;
Sow not these graves with dragon's teeth;
Part of England lies beneath
Both the granite and the loam:
Let the divided heart come home
To half-content, and understand
His passion for a wilder land
Still untamed and still unfed
By flesh and bone that England bred.
If we desert the deed undone
Alas, what daughter and what son!
Break the sword: the iron strike
To plough-shares, share and share alike!

Fabulous Ballad

A gypsy, who had lost a chain of beads
(Blue glass, they were, and threaded on a shoe-string),
Went round about the lanes in mourning weeds
Weeping her loss, and begging for a new string.

A lady, who inhabited a house
Known in those parts (perhaps) as Joyous Manor,
Walked through the dusk below laburnum boughs,
In gentleness and chastity and honour.

All praised her, from the potentates and kings
Down to the least of village dames and gaffers;
She had, among her several pretty things,
A delicate celestial chain of sapphires.

The lady's hair was like a golden fleece;
Like God's own mother she was clad in azure;
She read the curious history of Lucrece
And swung the sky, suspended in her treasure.

The gypsy, who had wandered to the edge
Of this domain, being blinded by her dolour,
Crawled like a weasel through the privet hedge,
And touched the chain, and kissed its heaven-colour.

The gypsy's hair was rusty like a rake
And crowned with straw, since straw had been her pillow;
Her brow was banded, for her sorrow's sake,
With plaited coronal of weeping-willow.

"Sweet Virgin" (so her sorrow turned her brain),
She cried; "be sure I have not come to pilfer;
I know in truth that this is not my chain;
My clasp was gold (I think) and yours is silver.

"But every link is lighter than a leaf
And fitly wrought to hold its proper jewel."
The lady, who was witness to her grief,
Offered her neither petticoats nor gruel.

The lady, who was witness to her tears,
Offered her neither sage advice nor question;
She said: "The moon is up; the weather clears."
She was a noble lady, and a Christian.

She said: "You shall be servant to this gem;
If it grow dull (or even slightly dullish),
Keep every flower upon its silver stem
A star, with chamois skin and goldsmith's polish."

The gypsy knelt upon the lilied ground,
Crouched, like a beast upon its silly haunches;
The lady said: " . . . Until your own is found
Whose clasp was brighter than laburnum branches."

Her lord, who late had left the garden close
Because the gardeners were burning rubbish,
Returned to smile, and then to look morose
(He was superior and slightly snobbish).

"My dear," he said, "I am the more amazed
To see you trust the drab with something precious,
Because, while this particular one is crazed,
All gypsies are dishonest and malicious."

"My dear," she said, "go seek upon your shelf
Corinthians, xiii; it cannot hurt you;
And leave this beggar-woman and myself
To love these stars' incomparable virtue."

Letter to V—

No, V—, you never will persuade me
That Death is other than a friend;
I can't believe the hand that made me
Shall so unmake me in the end.

Suppose a Holy Ghost or Spirit
Came dressed in red instead of white;
A child may see some such, and fear it
On Christmas Eve or Christmas night.

It's not a Dustman or a Reaper;
It's not a wormy skeleton;
Perhaps the dark disguise is deeper
But It's the Father or the Son.

You will not look, because you dassn't,
At what is hidden in His bag;
I know it is another Present;
Eagle's wing or skin of stag.

They call it Future, but it isn't;
It is the Present when it come;
And shall the swinging fruit be wizened?
And shall the singing bird be dumb?

You know, upon our birthday mornings,
They gave us pretty hair and eyes;
Why should our lives' entire earnings
Be less than excrement of flies?

It's not because I've had so little;
It is because I've had so much
That I believe that clay and spittle
Contain the soul of Such and Such

The secret—and He has not told it—
Is that which here escapes us most;
And, even though we try to hold it,
It shall not finally be lost.

Although they burn me on a faggot
I turn me to my Father's house;
I will not have Him called a Maggot;
I will not have Him called a Louse.

I will not have Him called a Nothing;
I'll love Him, and I'll lay me down,
In silver coverlid and clothing,
Beside my brother, Thomas Browne.

And, while I live, I'll call Him *Mighty*,
Yea, and *Eloquent* and *Just*;
And scratch in earth: *Integer Vitæ*;
And: *Dolce Mors* upon the dust.

The Pebble

If any have a stone to shy,
Let him be David and not I;
The lovely shepherd, brave and vain,
Who has a maggot in the brain,
Which, since the brain is bold and pliant,
Takes the proportions of a giant.
Alas, my legendary fate!
Who sometimes rage, but never hate.
Long, long before the pebble flieth
I see a virtue in Goliath;
Yea, in the Philistine his face,
A touching majesty and grace;
Then like the lights of evening shine
The features of the Philistine
Until my spirit faints to see
The beauty of my enemy.
If any have a stone to fling
Let him be a shepherd-king,
Who is himself so beautiful
He may detest the gross and dull
With holy rage and heavenly pride
To make a pebble sanctified
And feather its course with wings of scorn;
But, from the day that I was born
Until like corn I bow to the sickle,
I am in hatred false and fickle.
I am most cruel to anyone
Who hates me with devotion;
I will not freeze, I will not burn;
I make his heart a poor return

For all the passion that he spends
In swearing we shall never be friends;
For all the pains his passion spent
In hatred I am impotent;
The sad perversity of my mind
Sees in him my kin and kind.
Alas, my shameful heritage,
False in hate and fickle in rage!
Alas, to lack the power to loathe!
I like them each; I love them both;
Philistine and shepherd-king
They strike the pebble from my sling;
My heart grows cold, my spirit grows faint;
Behold, a hero and a saint
Where appeared, a moment since,
A giant and a heathen prince;
And I am bound and given over
To be no better than a lover.
Alas, who strove as a holy rebel!
They have broke my sling and stole my pebble:
If any have a stone to throw
It is not I, ever or now.

Country Song

Over by Peppard
A great light shone:
It looked to the shepherd
Like the setting sun.

It looked to the keeper
Like a bright cloud bank
That coloured deeper
The red deer's flank.

It looked to the miller
Where the mill race flowed
Like a tall gold pillar
Of fire and cloud.

It looked to the farmer
Like the sun through the trees
And the air grown warmer
That had seemed to freeze.

It looked to the ploughmen
And the takers-in of hay
Like the crystal omen
Of another clear day.

And it looked to the drover
Like a burning glass.
But only the lover
Knew what it was.

Sonnets

PASTICHE

Is not the woman moulded by your wish
A cockatrice of a most intricate kind?
You have, my friend, the high fantastic mind
To clasp the cold enamel of a fish
As breastplate for a bosom tigerish;
To make a dove a dragon; or to bind
A panther skin upon the escaping hind:
You mix ambiguous spices in your dish.

Will there remain, when this embellished I
Sprout wings, or am by cloven heels improved,
An atom of the lady that you loved?
Does Christ or Lucifer seal this alchemy?
Is there not lacking from your synthesis
Someone you may occasionally miss?

SONNET

You are the faintest freckles on the hide
Of fawns; the hoofprint stamped into the slope
Of slithering glaciers by the antelope;
The silk upon the mushroom's under side
Constricts you, and your eyelashes are wide
In pools uptilted on the hills; you grope
For swings of water twisted to a rope
Over a ledge where amber pebbles glide.

Shelley perceived you on the Caucasus;
Blake prisoned you in glassy grains of sand
And Keats in goblin jars from Samarcand;
Poor Coleridge found you in a poppy-seed;
But you escape the clutching most of us,
Shaped like a ghost, and imminent with speed.

SONNET

How many faults you might accuse me of
Are truth, and by my truthfulness admitted!
A fool, perhaps, how many caps had fitted,
How many motleys clothed me like a glove.
Thriftless of gold and prodigal of love;
Fanatical in pride, and feather-witted
In the world's business; if your tongue had spitted
Such frailties, they were possible to prove.

But you have hit the invulnerable joint
In this poor armour patched from desperate fears;
This is the breastplate that you cannot pierce,
That turns and breaks your most malicious point;
This strict ascetic habit of control
That industry has woven for my soul.

TO LLEWELYN,
WHO INQUIRED CONCERNING WYVERNS

Alas, in London, wyverns never dwell;
I have beheld them in a golden herd,
Mailed like a serpent, feathered like a bird,
Feeding on hawthorn and the faint bluebell,
The which they drink like water, and the smell
Of woodbine is their honey, and the curd
Of the white moonlight broken up and stirred
Serves them for delicate manna where it fell.

Alas, Llewelyn, they will not assault—
Having such heavenly business of their own—
These iron bars, these walls of stupid stone;
Do not upbraid them for their beauty's fault;
For when myself has freed me from this chain
They'll kiss my wounds, and comfort me again.

NON DISPUTANDUM

I'd rather be myself, to wear my knees
Fleshless with grovelling before my kind,
Wherefrom returns the image of a mind
Dimly augmented by nobilities,
Than own eleven silver palaces,
If, among all my vassals, I could find
No thief, or beggar lame and halt and blind,
But soiled my velvet with his dust and fleas.

I'd rather be a dog, and bay the moon,
Than such a Roman: O, I'd rather be
The unforgiven sinner on the Tree,
Or Peter, turned unfaithful at a pinch,
Than thrust red Lucifer, lost and overthrown,
Hell-deeper by the fraction of an inch!

BIRTHDAY SONNET

Take home Thy prodigal child, O Lord of Hosts!
Protect the sacred from the secular danger;
Advise her, that Thou never needst avenge her;
Marry her mind neither to man's nor ghost's
Nor holier domination's, if the costs
Of such commingling should transport or change her;
Defend her from familiar and stranger
And earth's and air's contagions and rusts.

Instruct her strictly to preserve Thy gift
And alter not its grain in atom sort;
Angels may wed her to their ultimate hurt
And men embrace a spectre in a shift
So that no drop of the pure spirit fall
Into the dust: defend Thy prodigal.

INDEX OF FIRST LINES

A NOTE ON THE TYPE

IN WHICH THIS BOOK IS SET

The letters of Nicholas Jenson served as a model to Bruce Rogers in cutting the Centaur type in which this book is set. It was a desire to improve on the cutting of his earlier type called Montaigne, and to effect a refinement in it that led to the cutting of the Centaur. The headings are set in Arrighi Italic designed by Frederic Warde.

Composed at The Lakeside Press, Chicago